THE BIRTH OF
ROCK 'N' ROLL

THE BIRTH OF
ROCK 'N' ROLL

THE ILLUSTRATED STORY
OF SUN RECORDS

AND THE 70 RECORDINGS THAT CHANGED THE WORLD

PETER GURALNICK AND **COLIN ESCOTT**

FOREWORD BY
JERRY LEE LEWIS

weldonowen

CONTENTS

FOREWORD

Above: Jerry Lee Lewis and Sam Phillips.

When I first heard about Sam Phillips and Sun Records, I knew if I could play for Sam he could make me a star; he was the man I needed to see to really get things going. He'd already made Elvis a hit, and if he could do it for Elvis he could certainly do it for Jerry Lee Lewis. My daddy sold thirty-three dozen eggs so he could drive me from Ferriday, Louisiana, to Memphis, Tennessee, just so I could audition for Sam. I was determined to get him to hear my music, but when we arrived he was out of town, so I auditioned for "Cowboy" Jack Clement. I made Jack promise to play my audition for Sam, and when he did Sam knew what I knew—which is that I was going all the way to the top.

Some of the best days of my life were spent recording at Sun. It was much different back then than it is today. To cut a record today you need thirty people, but back in those days we would just show up and let 'er rip. Sam didn't want to record "Whole Lot of Shakin' Going On" at first. He wanted me to record "It'll Be Me" instead, which I did, but that wasn't what people wanted to hear. They wanted to hear real rock 'n' roll. I kept after Sam until he agreed to do it. We cut "Whole Lot of Shakin' Going On" just like we'd done it onstage, something that would never happen today. When it came out, I was right: It was what the people wanted to hear. It was real rock 'n' roll, and that's what we did at Sun: We cut real rock 'n' roll records. That was the beginning of it all. Rock 'n' roll started at Sun Records, and without Sun there would be no rock 'n' roll.

Elvis asked me how I was possibly going to follow up "Whole Lot of Shakin' Going On." Well, I wasn't too worried about that so I just turned to him and said, "Oh, I'll think of something," and walked away. Of course we followed up with "Great Balls of Fire," which we originally recorded for a movie called *Jamboree*. If you watch that movie you'll notice "Great Balls of Fire" is a different cut than on the record. I didn't feel like that original take was quite right. It was good but I knew it could be better. We took that song back to the studio at Sun, recut it, and the rest is history.

A lot of people have asked me over the years what I think of Sam Phillips. It's sure that we didn't always see eye to eye, but you know, he was like a brother to me. He helped me get my start, and for that I will forever be grateful. There will never be another like him and there will never be another Sun Records. That's where it all started, with Sam, Carl Perkins, Roy Orbison, Johnny Cash, and of course, ole Jerry Lee. Sam Phillips and Sun Records changed the whole world.

I can't believe it's been seventy years since Sam founded Sun Records, and I'm blessed to be here to celebrate it with my fans, Sam's fans, Sun Records' fans. God bless you all.

—Jerry Lee Lewis

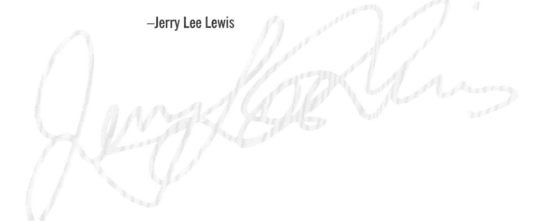

Monday, November 21, 1955. Elvis officially signs with
RCA Victor. From left: Elvis's manager-of-record, Bob
Neal; Sam Phillips; RCA attorney H. Coleman Tily; Elvis;
Elvis's new de facto manager Colonel Parker.

THE HISTORY OF SUN RECORDS,
PART I: BY COLIN ESCOTT
1952-1969

PROLOGUE, PART I:
SAM PHILLIPS AND THE MEMPHIS RECORDING SERVICE

The music business needs visionaries, eccentrics, and true believers to see past the distraction, ignore the background noise, and find something that wasn't there before. Bring it to those who need to hear it. In finding it, they find themselves. The Chess brothers, Leonard and Phil, born in a shtetl in what is now Belarus, learned to differentiate between okay, good, and extraordinary blues. A Black Detroit auto line worker, Berry Gordy, brought the assembly line to R&B, making records for all of "Young America." Ahmet Ertegun, son of the Turkish ambassador to the United States, became a shrewd judge of almost anything with its roots in American Black music. Born into Vanderbilt money, John Hammond signed artists of singular vision from Billie Holiday to Bob Dylan and Bruce Springsteen. London-born Don Law assembled perhaps the richest ever roster in country music. And a farm kid from Florence, Alabama, who harbored dreams of being a defense attorney, saw what Elvis Presley, Johnny Cash, and Jerry Lee Lewis could be.

Samuel Cornelius Phillips was born on a farm in northwest Alabama in 1923. With cotton prices declining since World War I, the Great Depression was almost old news to Alabama farmers. Poverty shaped Phillips. "As a child I was all ears more than eyes. The way people said things gave an almost instant insight into that individual and what they were confronted with each morning. Now, people may not think this is highly important to music. I got news for you. It is singularly the most important ingredient into creativity."

The youngest child with a solitary disposition, Phillips became an adult with many acquaintances but few friends. Unable to realize his dream of law school, he became a radio announcer and engineer. Radio took him to Decatur, Alabama, and then Nashville. Shortly after leaving for Decatur, he got married. One year into his marriage, the anxiety disorder and depression that had bedeviled him for years led to hospitalization and treatment with electroconvulsive therapy. He never talked about it in this way, but perhaps his own proximity to the edge led him to look into others' eyes with compassion and insight.

In 1945, Phillips moved to Memphis. It had been his celestial city since he'd driven there in 1939 en route to a revival in Dallas. Around four o'clock in the morning, he was on Beale Street, known then as the "Main Street of Negro America." "It was *rockin'*," he said, reliving that slow crawl down Beale's fifteen blocks. "It was so active—musically, socially. God, I loved it!" He became an on-air personality and engineer at radio station WREC. "I had a notion [about] Memphis and its potential in music. Never has there been a greater symphony in the world than the symphony of the soul. Impoverished, but blessed with hardship and then telling about it in song. Anybody that has missed the profound statements of Black music, Southern White music, I feel sorry for them. I was lucky enough to be brought to this place and to these people, and to these experiences."

Memphis had one professional-quality studio, Royal Recording, run by Jerry Thompson, an engineer at radio station WHHM. It started in 1947 but was out of business by 1949. "It was because of the closure of Royal that my bosses at WREC warned me against trying to start my

Above: Sam Phillips, c. 1945.

Oppposite: The Memphis Recording Service soon after it opened in January 1950.

own recording business," Phillips said later. But in October 1949, he signed a lease on a small storefront at 706 Union Avenue, in the heart of what was called the automobile district, and began building a studio: the Memphis Recording Service.

It's the Phillips

Several months after opening the Memphis Recording Service, Phillips secured a deal with Bill McCall's 4 Star and Gilt-Edge Records in Pasadena, California. McCall cut similar deals across the country. For a flat fee he bought all rights, including the music publishing, in perpetuity. That way he ended up with songs such as "Release Me," as well as Patsy Cline's earliest records and much more. Phillips supplied McCall with some R&B and country recordings before realizing that—green as he was in the business—there was only one winner in a McCall deal.

Around the same time, Phillips partnered with Memphis's premier R&B disc jockey, Dewey Phillips, on a label called It's the Phillips. The tagline, "Hottest Thing in the Country," was one of Dewey's catchphrases, misapplied here. Sam and Dewey pressed an estimated three hundred copies of one record by blues singer Joe Hill Louis, "Gotta Let You Go" (*see p. 64*), and quite probably failed to sell out the run.

A little earlier, Phillips had met Jules, Joe, and Saul Bihari, who were looking for studio time to record their new artist, B. B. King. The Los Angeles-based Biharis wanted Southern repertoire

Right: Dewey Phillips was Sam Phillips's "brother from another mother." His nightly R&B show on WHBQ had a broad cross-racial audience, especially among teenagers. He became a local tastemaker and kingmaker.

Below: An early note from the desk of Sam Phillips. Sam never missed an opportunity to call attention to his earliest discoveries.

Left: Beale Street, corner of Second Street. The Blue Light Studio took the first publicity photos of several Sun artists.

Talent Just waiting
To be discovered
Jackie Brenston
B.B. King
Joe Hill Louis
Rufus Thomas
Ike Turner
Howling Wolf
Phineas Newborn
+ others

for their RPM and Modern Records labels. They liked Phillips, and to him they epitomized the freewheeling glamor of the postwar record business. The relationship lasted until mid-1951, when they fell out over Jackie Brenston's "Rocket '88' (*see p. 57*). The Biharis felt that they had first call on it, but Phillips secured a sweeter deal from Chess Records in Chicago, and continued to supply masters to Chess for another year or two.

In licensing to other labels, Phillips thought he could focus on capturing music without having to deal with the nuts and bolts of airplay, distribution, and so on. It wasn't long before he was once again toying with the idea of starting his own label, but to hear him tell it, Sun was a decision almost foisted upon him.

1952

THE SUN RISES

Above: Rosco Gordon, inviting everyone to get "Booted."

Below: The Memphis Recording Service tote bag. After Elvis Presley made his first personal recording, he probably carried it home in a bag like this.

Opposite: SUN 175, the first official Sun recording.

By early 1952, Phillips was at a crossroads. It had been just over two years since he'd opened the Memphis Recording Service. Some days it must have seemed as if a lifetime's highs, lows, and in-betweens had been compacted into those months. He had recorded one of the era's biggest R&B hits, "Rocket '88'," and as soon as he heard Howlin' Wolf (*see p. 63*), he knew he'd found greatness. He was becoming known within the small, fiercely rivalrous R&B record business. He'd suffered a nervous breakdown. He'd quit his day job, but his only reliable source of income was recording weddings, funerals, and commercials—exactly what he did not want to do. Through it all, he was convinced that he was in the right place, even if he alone saw it. No other studios or record companies were headquartered in Memphis.

In February 1952, it all came to a head. The Chess brothers were probably telling Phillips that he had the best deal an independent producer could get. It was certainly good for the Chesses. Following Brenston and Wolf, Phillips's newest discovery, Rosco Gordon, was licensed to Chess, and Gordon's record "Booted" was closing in on the top of the R&B chart. The Biharis took revenge for losing out on Brenston, Gordon, and Wolf by surreptitiously recording Wolf and Gordon, and by hiring Brenston's bandleader, Ike Turner, as their man in the mid-South.

In a deal announced in mid-February 1952, the Biharis and Chesses reached an accommodation over Phillips's artists. Brenston's stock had fallen but he would remain on Chess, for whatever that was worth. Gordon went to the Biharis while Howlin' Wolf went to Chess. It was probably assumed that Phillips would continue to produce Wolf while giving Chess the first option on anyone else he discovered.

By the time that deal was announced, Phillips's ambivalence about working for others was becoming pretty clear. The rewards seemed incommensurate with the success, and there was a nagging suspicion that he had not received a full accounting from either the Biharis or Chesses.

On February 23, Phillips recorded a singing deejay from Forrest City, Arkansas, Walter Bradford. Two days later he recorded a duo, Jack Kelly and Walter Horton. Kelly was a veteran of the Memphis blues scene who had recorded before World War II. Horton was an up-and-coming harmonica player whom Phillips had recorded for the Biharis. Phillips began thinking that perhaps he should issue these himself.

On March 1, Phillips recorded a teenage alto saxophonist, Johnny London. Phillips sent a copy to Chess. One song, "Drivin' Slow" (*see p. 69*), was rerecorded on March 8. Perhaps Chess said no; perhaps Phillips withdrew the option. Fired up by the rerecording of "Drivin' Slow," Phillips sent a dub to late-night R&B deejay Ruby Hudson at Memphis's WHHM, asking her to air it as the "intro to the new Sun label." He was having second thoughts about the Bradford and Kelly-Horton recordings, but ordered pressings of Johnny London. With one thousand records on his distributor's floor as of March 27, Sun Records was born. If Phillips checked the trade magazines, he would have found no reviews of London's disc, but a few weeks earlier he might have seen a review of a record by Don Paull and the Canyon Caravan on Sun Records . . . in Albuquerque, New Mexico.

Sun did not take flight in 1952. Phillips had only local distribution. If he sampled London's record to stations outside Memphis, few if any picked up on it. Sun went dormant for nine months. A local label was impracticable, Phillips concluded. Talking to *Mix* magazine in 2004, he explained, "You might not have the power of distribution that the majors had, but you had to get out of a region and expose records to enough people." Today, hip-hop and R&B are two of music's most popular genres, but in 1952, R&B sales reportedly totaled less than kiddie discs. Phillips was chasing a tiny piece of a small market.

Nashville record man Jim Bulleit came in as Phillips's partner. Bulleit knew the business side—manufacturing, distribution, taxes, and so on. By January 1953, when Sun was relaunched, they had distributors in all the markets where R&B sold well. By then, the Sun label in New Mexico had been persuaded to relinquish the name. Of more concern was the arrival of two new R&B labels in Memphis, one of them owned by the fourth Bihari brother, Lester. Phillips no longer had Memphis to himself.

Bulleit didn't stick around, but Sun limped on in 1953 through cash-flow problems and self-inflicted injuries. Whatever joy Phillips took from his first Sun hit, Rufus Thomas's "Bear Cat," was dented by a lawsuit (*see p. 75*). His star vocal group, the Prisonaires (*see pp. 83, 91*), weren't prisoners of love but of the Tennessee penal system, and thus couldn't tour to support their records. His first thirty-five releases were predominantly blues and R&B, but White gospel

> "*You might not have the power of distribution that the majors had, but you had to get out of a region and expose records to enough people.*"
>
> —Sam Phillips

"It was then a word-of-mouth thing among Black musicians, where they realized that here was a studio that would actually try to do something to get their music exposed. ... They found out that I not only worked hard with them, but that I enjoyed it, appreciated their music, and would not let them try to please me by playing what they thought a White man wanted."—Sam Phillips

Right: Lester Bihari with his assistant Leona Wynn, Meteor Records studio, mid-1950s.

Left: Sam Phillips at his recording console.

singers, a Black gospel quartet, a couple of hillbilly bands, and an anemic pop singer figured into the mix. Among those scattershot releases were some of the era's finest blues records.

In September 1953, Associated Press stringer Bill Crider reported on the Prisonaires' second Sun session. He seemed nearly incredulous that Phillips, a "thin, wiry blue-eyed [i.e. White] man," was drawn to this music. "He has specialized in off-beat race records for three years. Raw jazz, dusky blues, rhythmic spirituals, and shoutin' boogie are his life. He gives a cottonpatch original the same close hearing as Tin Pan Alley would accord Cole Porter's latest." And how percipient that seems now. Phillips, said Crider, "treats his artists with easy humor and understanding. When they're broke, he feeds them. When the situation warrants, he loans money against future earnings." And then the kicker: as wards of the state, the Prisonaires "have no concern about eating regularly."

Other labels might do two takes and call it a day, but Phillips would sit behind the console until dawn if he thought he might capture the moment it all jelled. That Prisonaires' session lasted fourteen hours. Virtuosity didn't impress Phillips; in fact, Crider reported Phillips's frustration at the Prisonaires' insistence upon faultlessness. "What's the matter? It sounded good." Phillips's assistant, Marion Keisker, remarked that he was by nature an impatient person who had bottomless patience in this one sphere. Years later, explaining what he was looking for, Phillips could tie himself up with circumlocutions. It was a different story when he sat behind the console in the 1950s. He was drawn to simplicity because it left nowhere to hide. He wanted to feel one soul touching another. He found it in the blues and country music. And soon, rock 'n' roll.

CREATING THE SUN LABEL

Left to right:

SUN 175
The first label.

SUN 232
Color variations.

SUN 245
Sacrificing the rooster.

SUN 1107
Shelby adds the bullseye.

"The sun to me, even as a kid back on the farm, was a universal kind of thing. A new day, a new opportunity," Sam Phillips reflected later.

When Sun started, most nonclassical music was sold on ten-inch discs that played at seventy-eight revolutions per minute. These 78s had been the predominant sound carrier for decades. A three-and-a-half-inch-diameter label was affixed to the record when it was still a molten compound on the press.

Phillips's first one-off venture into the record business, It's the Phillips, sported a crudely stenciled design. Sun's records needed to reflect Phillips's reborn self-belief. He'd recorded hits for other companies and better understood how to capture music that would sell and be truthful.

Back in Florence, Phillips had known a graphic artist, Jay Parker, who'd moved to Memphis one year after him. Parker worked at Memphis Engraving, one block from the Peabody Hotel, where Phillips worked in the basement studio of radio station WREC. In Parker's account, he ran into Phillips one morning at a nearby restaurant, where they were both getting breakfast. Phillips remembered it differently (but perhaps not inconsistently), saying that he took a rough sketch to Memphis Engraving and was directed to Parker's office, only to find that they knew each other.

Phillips laid out his vision for the label artwork. Parker had never designed a record label but submitted several comps, and Phillips chose one with a rooster crowing at dawn's first rays. Fleshing it out, Parker drew musical notes on a staff circling most of the perimeter. The notes were, in Parker's words, "thrown in as gingerbread." He remembered charging about fifty dollars for the comps and the finished artwork. To keep Phillips's costs down, Parker chose one color, brown, to print on gold or yellow labels. Through the years,

depending on the printer, the label backgrounds ranged in color from lemon to amber. The print was meant to be tawny or rust brown, but it varied too. "We never changed [the design] when [others] had these labels with ten different beautiful colors, we just stuck by our little, simple label," Phillips said later.

Rock 'n' roll was the first music to be played primarily at 45 RPM. Introduced in 1949, 45s were relatively unbreakable. Just seven inches in diameter, they were pressed on a lighter compound than 78s. There was still a three-and-a-half-inch-diameter label, but a one-and-a-half-inch spindle hole was dinked out of the center so that the singles could be stacked on a new generation of auto-change record players. The rooster had to go. "That really hurt," Phillips said later.

Phillips could have reintroduced the rooster when he began issuing LPs in 1956, but chose not to. Never a strong believer in albums, Phillips thought of singles, whether 78s or 45s, as the consummate musical artifact. He issued more than three hundred singles on Sun and its affiliated labels, but just twenty albums.

Under Shelby Singleton's stewardship, four target-like circles were dropped into the Sun label background and the rooster stayed gone. Within one year, Singleton had issued more albums than Phillips had issued in ten.

Today, the Sun logo is emblazoned upon a wide range of merchandise, more visible than at any time in its seventy years.

And Jay Parker? He created designs for Alka-Seltzer, Super Bubble bubble gum, and the Cincinnati Bengals football team. Later he taught art and design at Memphis State University and became an amateur watercolorist. He died in 2012.

"The sun to me, even as a kid back on the farm, was a universal kind of thing. A new day, a new opportunity."

—Sam Phillips

1954

THE ARRIVAL OF ELVIS

On Monday, July 5, 1954, Elvis Presley came to Sun to record a country love song. He'd been in twice before to record personal discs. Phillips had taken note of him and invited him to try out with a pair of musicians from Doug Poindexter's country band. He gave them a song and told them to come back when they'd worked it up. During a break, Elvis unaccountably cut loose on an eight-year-old blues tune, "That's All Right" (*see p. 115*). Very few other record-label owners would have even let a kid who had hardly performed outside his bedroom into the studio, let alone spend hours with him. Surely, no one else would have instantly recognized that this kid singing the blues song was the way forward. Nothing like "That's All Right" was selling or had ever sold, but Phillips didn't care. It felt good to him, and he released it. He realized what he was hearing and imagined what it could be. No one can take that away from him. He remembered Paul Ackerman at *Billboard* magazine telling him, "Sam, you have to be crazy or the most brilliant person in the world. Did you not know what you were doing?" Phillips recalled, "I said, 'Hell, no.' It came together. It didn't have to have a color. It didn't need one."

Presley's music might not need a color, but it needed a category. Phillips pitched him to country radio and country show bookers. Pop music usually meant forty-piece orchestras. R&B was almost exclusively the domain of Black artists and Black audiences. For the seventeen months that he was on Sun, Elvis Presley was perceived and marketed as a country singer. Country music was made with tavern jukeboxes in mind, but Presley appealed to a younger generation of country music fans. It was new music for a largely unexplored market.

Phillips couldn't deconstruct the music he wanted to hear and explain its constituent parts to musicians. He just simply knew when he heard it. Presley was it. Even better, Presley sold records. Not the millions he would sell on RCA, but more than Phillips had ever sold before. The problem was that small labels relied upon independent distributors and pressing plants. Hits were often the worst thing that could happen. Labels had to collect from distributors in time to pay plants, freight companies, wages, and royalties. Distributors would often pay just enough not to be cut off, or they'd pay for today's hits with yesterday's unsold merchandise. That was the squeeze. Phillips needed capital to get over that hump.

Phillips's exasperation poured out in a letter to his brother, Jud, to whom he owed money: "I have told you repeatedly that Sun liabilities are three times the assets and I have been making every effort possible to stay out of bankruptcy. As you well know, we have had only Presley and with his Union contract of 3% of the 89¢ price, plus the fact that the songs cost 4¢ a record, it has been virtually impossible to make anything . . . I intend to pay every dollar the company owes even while I know there is no possible way to come out with a dollar."

Knowing Phillips's predicament, major labels came calling. Was the kid available? Phillips was pretty sure that Presley would leave when his deal was up, and knew that Sun might well go broke before then, so he negotiated with RCA. "I made a damn proposition I didn't think they'd take," he said. "I didn't think they'd be fool enough to take it, and it was the eleventh hour before they *did* take it. The price [$35,000] doesn't sound like anything today, but what I needed was the money just so I could get on the mound and throw to a batter."

Below: Elvis returns to Sun, September 23, 1956, for Marion Keisker's thirty-ninth birthday.

Left: Sam Phillips with his mastering lathe, while Elvis, Bill Black (center), and Scotty Moore (right) look on. Early 1955.

> "I didn't think they'd be fool enough to take it, and it was the eleventh hour before they did *take it.*"
>
> —Sam Phillips

"COWBOY" JACK CLEMENT

Sound engineer, studio owner, musician, songwriter, producer, film-maker, dance instructor, label owner, radio host, music publisher, sage, and mentor. Jack Clement was all those. His Cowboy Arms Hotel and Recording Spa was just a few blocks down Nashville's Belmont Boulevard from Shelby Singleton's building. Singleton's offices were usually vacated by 5 p.m., but the Cowboy Arms might be just springing to life by then. Clement held court, often at his desk with his 1952 Gibson J-200 hanging on the wall behind him. He'd played it on several Sun recordings, most memorably Johnny Cash's "Big River" (*see p. 183*). He was always quotable: "I've got a bunch of people who say I'm a genius. That don't make me one, but you've got to be pretty smart to get all them people to say that." His rules for success in the music business concluded with, "When all else fails, get lucky."

Born in the Memphis suburb of Whitehaven in 1931, Clement joined the US Marines in 1948 and began playing bluegrass when he was stationed in Washington, DC. Out of the service, he worked in the thriving DC-area bluegrass scene. Back in Memphis by 1954, he went to college and worked as an Arthur Murray dance instructor. Even in his later, overweight years he moved with grace. He took a record he'd produced in a garage studio to Sam Phillips, and was offered a job as Phillips's assistant. "He was so unconventional," Phillips said later. "I could see it in his eyes."

Clement joined Sun on June 15, 1956, working first with Roy Orbison. In December, when Phillips was out of town, Clement recorded a demo session with Jerry Lee Lewis, and later wrote the B side of Lewis's first hit, "Whole Lot of Shakin' Going On." Lewis would probably have finagled his way into Sun anyway, but Clement instantly recognized that Phillips needed to hear him.

By the end of 1957, Phillips was entrusting Clement with his marquee artist, Johnny Cash. Phillips wanted to reinvigorate Cash's sales with a fresh perspective. Clement believed that Sun's output was primitive, unmusical. He tried to change that, prettifying Cash's sound by introducing choruses and pop songs. Statistically, "Ballad of a Teenage Queen" (*see p. 115*) and "Guess Things Happen That Way" (*see p. 186*), both written and produced by Clement, were Cash's highest-charting records on Sun. Cash, though, rarely performed them later in his career, so they don't figure prominently in his story.

Phillips fired Clement in February 1959. There had been an argument, but the underlying cause was probably that Sun's fortunes were declining and Phillips likely felt that Clement wasn't doing enough to reverse the slide. Clement had even released two records under his own name and another as the Clement Travelers. No sales there, either.

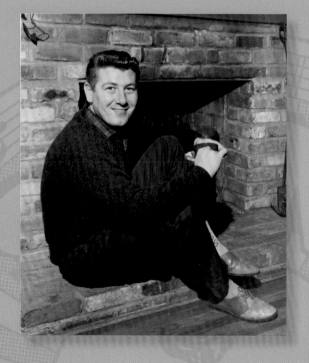

Clement started his own label and studio in Memphis, then spent a few frustrating months working for RCA's Nashville division before going to Beaumont, Texas, to build another studio and start a publishing company. Although scared of horses, he acquired the nickname "Cowboy." On one of several trips to Nashville, he produced Cash's "Ring of Fire" for Columbia Records, and he relocated there permanently in 1965. His big coup was selling RCA on Charley Pride. As part of the deal, he produced nearly all of Pride's biggest hits. Setting up another label, JMI, he signed Don Williams, producing Williams's earliest hits. In 1974 he produced the album that's widely considered to be Waylon

Jack Clement, hard at work at his desk at Sun studio.

Jennings's best, *Dreaming My Dreams*. Later, he produced some of the tracks for U2's *Rattle and Hum* at the old Sun studio.

The Cowboy Arms became the closest Nashville ever got, or needed to get, to a Parisian salon. It was where an unknown songwriter would be on an equal footing with Johnny Cash.

Clement and Phillips engaged in epic late-night phone calls. Clement conceded that he had probably been misguided in trying to steer Sun uptown. "I was into making things musical," he said later. "Sam was not, but he understood one thing that I didn't at that time. He understood 'feel' in music." Clement died in August 2013, ten years after Phillips. Earlier that year, a tribute concert was held to honor him. Charley Pride, Kris Kristofferson, Dan Auerbach, John Prine, and many others performed and spoke both of him and to him. At the end, Clement rose to the stage. He performed a few songs, closing with the Rolling Stones' "No Expectations" (". . . to pass through here again").

"He was so unconventional. I could see it in his eyes."
—Sam Phillips

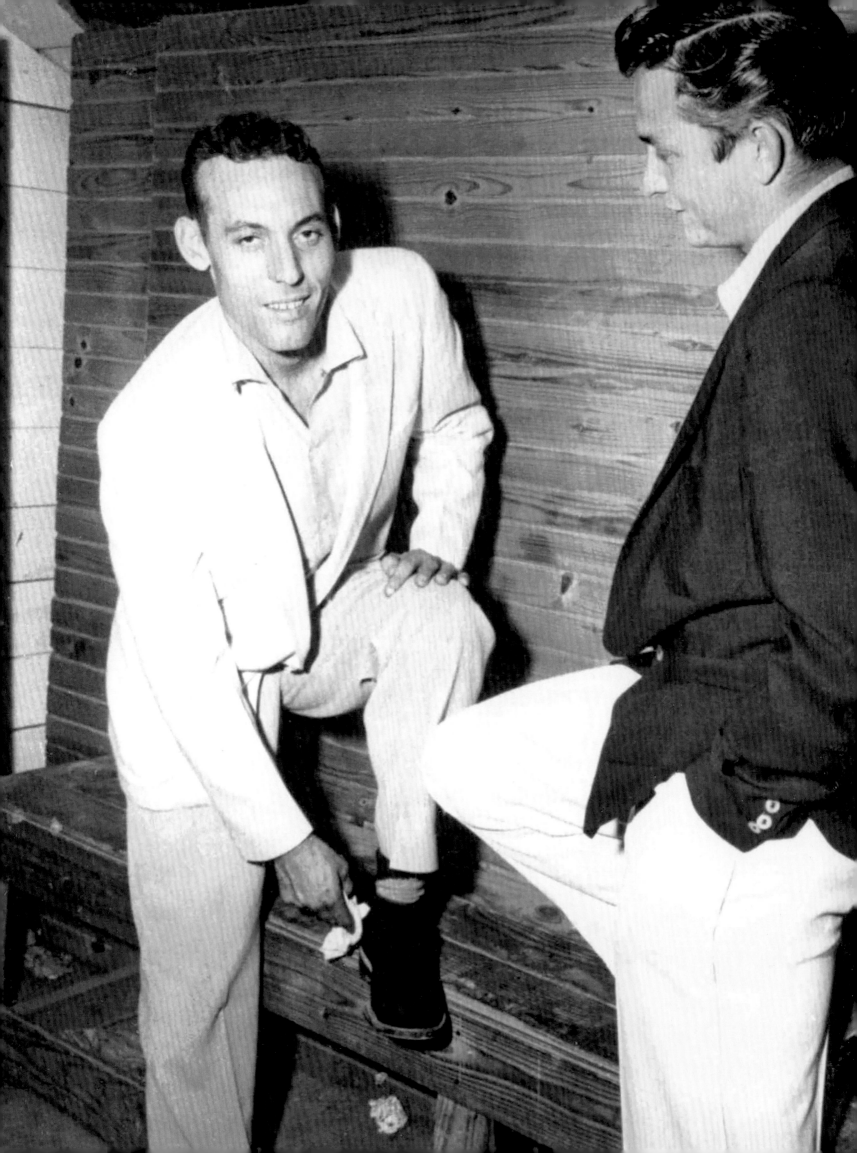

1956

JOHNNY, CARL, AND JERRY LEE

On November 21, 1955, Elvis Presley posed for a photo with Sam Phillips and RCA's legal counsel, H. Coleman Tily. His current and future managers, Bob Neal and Colonel Tom Parker, were there too. Running the photo and the story two weeks later, one of the industry's trade magazines, *Cash Box*, noted, "Presley has been the rage of the country bobby-soxers [industry shorthand for teenage country music fans]. In addition, the chanter has been a double threat on wax inasmuch as his platters have rhythm 'n' blues flavoring, and it's possible the versatile Presley could well become a big pop name."

With that, Presley was gone, but just as he had walked in, Phillips was confident others would follow. Johnny Cash and Carl Perkins were already there. Phillips recorded Perkins's "Blue Suede Shoes" (*see p. 136*) shortly after Presley left. Perkins's record and Presley's first RCA single, "Heartbreak Hotel," chased each other up the charts—the pop chart, the R&B chart, and the country chart, just as *Cash Box* foretold. Phillips was spectacularly vindicated. The reel of tape and perhaps the bottle of bourbon he'd invested in the session, together with some RCA capital to cover the gap between pressing and payment, paid a dividend more handsome than anything he'd dared dream. He was recording music no one else would have touched, he was recording it his way, he was releasing it on his own label, and he was about to reap the stupendous rewards.

Carl Perkins dusts off his blue suede shoes as Johnny Cash looks on. Mid-1956.

Perkins could never recapture the success of "Blue Suede Shoes," but Johnny Cash became Phillips's most consistent seller, even after he'd left the label. Phillips's immediate insight was that Cash's voice needed no more ornamentation than his ragged two-piece band provided. Lots of singers had deep voices, but Cash sang with heart-stopping conviction. Tenderness, empathy, boastfulness, wry humor, pathos, grit, and much more spilled from his records. Unlike 1940s country star Ernest Tubb, whose deep-voiced minimalism served as a beacon in some ways, Cash didn't go for ironic detachment.

The blues had taught Phillips how to frame what he was hearing. Audio experimentation had shown him how to capture it. On Sun, Cash's voice had a halo—the richness of a concert hall offset by the sibilance and slight distortion of a honky-tonk PA system. "Nashville in 1955 was grinding out all these country records," Cash wrote later, "and if you took the voice off, all the tracks sounded the same. It's kinda that way with my music, but at least it's my music." Phillips echoed that. "Can you imagine 'I Walk the Line' [*see p. 147*] with a steel guitar?" he once asked rhetorically. No vocalist benefited more from Phillips's tape echo or his insistence on stripping a performance to its essence.

Unlike most of his contemporaries at Sun, Cash was a restless autodidact, seemingly always on a quest. At the beginning of his career, he wore two-tone shoes, bolo ties, and fluted stage jackets. He smiled a lot and did a pretty good Elvis spoof. But he was an astute observer. One of his buddies, Merle Kilgore (who cowrote "Ring of Fire" and was the best man at Cash's marriage to June Carter), remembered Cash telling him to observe the stars: how they walked, how they cultivated and maintained an image, and how they differentiated themselves. Seeing that nearly everyone was wearing similar outfits, Cash adopted a different persona. He went to Memphis photographer William Speer, who loved the dramatic Rembrandt lighting of 1930s movie stills. Speer helped Cash recast his image. Phillips, though, was entrusting Cash to producer-songwriter Jack Clement, and the songs that Clement brought to the table took Cash in the opposite direction. It was one reason that Cash began to think that Sun was not the right place. A mythic place in retrospect, but perhaps not for him.

Phillips had no inkling of Cash's unease. In November 1956, he took a brief vacation in Florida, returning to find a demo tape of Jerry Lee Lewis that Clement had recorded in his

Left: Johnny Cash before the "Man in Black" look ...

...and after his makeover (right).

Below: Sam's hunch about Jerry Lee was right: Here a telegram announces him the Most Promising Country Male Vocalist of 1957 by Cash Box *magazine.*

Left: For the back liner of Jerry Lee Lewis's first Sun LP, he poses in the studio with Sam Phillips. Mid-1957.

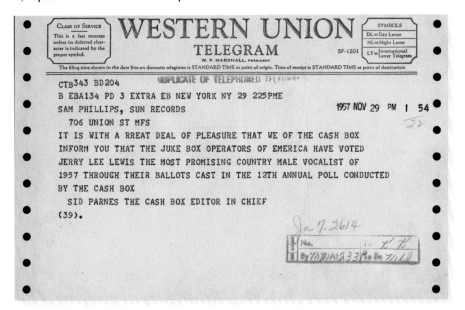

absence. "I don't know if I'd told Jack this," Phillips said later, "but I had been wanting to get off this guitar scene and show that it could be done with other instruments. They put that tape on and I said, 'Where in hell did this man come from?' He played that piano with abandon. A lot of people do that but I could hear, between the stuff that he played and didn't play, that spiritual thing. I told Jack, 'Just get him in here as fast as you can.'" Phillips released the first Jerry Lee Lewis record, "Crazy Arms," on December 1, 1956 (*see p. 167*).

Letting Lewis play song after song from his capacious memory, Phillips stumbled on Lewis's second record, "Whole Lot of Shakin' Going On" (*see p. 172*). The record's impact was felt far beyond the United States. "I was walking through Pontypridd where I come from in south Wales," remembered Tom Jones, "and I was with some of my friends and we were talking about rock 'n' roll and all of a sudden 'Whole Lot of Shakin'' comes out of the loudspeaker outside of the record shop and my friend said, 'Is that what you're talking about?' and I said, 'That's exactly what I'm talking about!'"

"They put that tape on and I said, 'Where in hell did this man come from?' He played that piano with abandon."

—Sam Phillips

THE MILLION DOLLAR QUARTET SESSION

Right: Elvis and Sam Phillips with Sun artist Smokey Joe Baugh.

Far right: The Million Dollar Quartet. From left: Jerry Lee Lewis, Carl Perkins, Elvis Presley, Johnny Cash.

These days, superstar get-togethers are almost invariably midwifed by managers, labels, networks, or corporate sponsors. The Million Dollar Quartet session was serendipity more than staging, but still had an element of intent.

On Tuesday, December 4, 1956, Sam Phillips and Jack Clement were behind the glass for a Carl Perkins session. Jerry Lee Lewis, trying to earn some money for Christmas, was the pianist. His first single had been out for several days. Sun's notoriously sloppy record-keeping means that we can only rely on our ears to tell us what was recorded, although "Matchbox" (*see p. 169*) and a "Blue Suede Shoes" knockoff, "Put Your Cat Clothes On," are good bets.

As the session wound down, Elvis Presley appeared with a small entourage. He picked up a guitar and—for love, not money—began to sing. Perkins's band joined him. Phillips realized that an event was unfolding and called Johnny Cash. He made another call across the road to the *Memphis Press-Scimitar*. Entertainment reporter Bob Johnson came over with a staff photographer, George B. Pierce, and the head of UPI's Memphis bureau, Leo Soroka.

Thirteen months earlier, Phillips had sold Presley's contract to RCA, plowing some of the proceeds into Cash and Perkins. Presley had become the most celebrated, vilified, and polarizing personality in American entertainment, selling one-half of all the records that RCA pressed in 1956. Perkins was trying to recapture the success he'd found in the early months of the year with "Blue Suede Shoes." Almost overnight, Cash had become one of country music's biggest

stars, earning an invitation to the Grand Ole Opry—an invitation that often took years to earn. Lewis was determined not to be overshadowed by the company in which he found himself.

Five future Rock & Roll Hall of Fame members in the same room should have ensured a rock concert like no other. Instead, the session was more a rough encapsulation of rock 'n' roll's roots: Southern gospel, Black gospel, country music, doo-wop, blues, and pop.

In his brief article, Johnson coined the phrase "Million Dollar Quartet." "If Sam Phillips had been on his toes," he added, "he'd have turned the recorder on. . . . That quartet could sell a million." Johnson, of course, probably knew that Phillips had done just that. Phillips and Clement rolled tape, but captured more of a $750,000 trio than a million dollar quartet, as Cash couldn't be heard. It's hard to know if Cash was far off mic or if he left before tape rolled. When Johnson wrote about the impromptu concert, he mentioned some songs that never made it to tape and spoke of Cash singing them, so the best guess is that Cash was there for a time, but left.

Phillips mimeographed the article and circulated it to deejays, appending a little postscript in his florid handwriting: "We thought you might like to read first-hand about our little shindig—it was a dilly!"

Poor-quality versions of some songs began appearing surreptitiously around 1980, but their provenance is unknown. It seems that Phillips made copies of the tapes, but it wasn't until the early 2000s that RCA producer Ernst Mikael Jorgensen found three reels at Graceland and restored them for release in 2006.

Twenty years after the session, RCA moved a portable recording studio to Graceland just in case Presley felt like recording something, anything. In 1956, he needed no encouragement to pick up a guitar and sing all night. "That's why I hate to get started in these jam sessions," he said. "I'm always the last to leave."

"If Sam Phillips had been on his toes, he'd have turned the recorder on. . . . That quartet could sell a million."

—Robert Johnson, *Memphis Press-Scimitar*, December 5, 1956

Above: Elvis with Johnny in the background.

Left (l-r): Carl, Elvis, and Johnny.

Bob Johnson, who coined *"Million Dollar Quartet"* (left), with Elvis, Sam Phillips, and UPI's Memphis bureau chief, Leo Soroka.

"We thought you might like to read first-hand about our little shindig— it was a dilly!"

—Sam Phillips

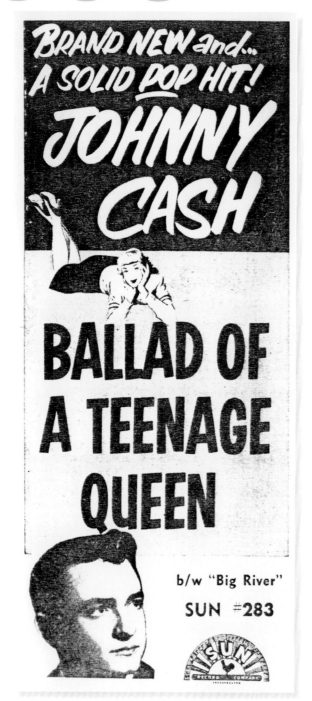

BRAND NEW and...
A SOLID POP HIT!
JOHNNY CASH
BALLAD OF A TEENAGE QUEEN
b/w "Big River"
SUN #283

Jerry Lee Lewis wasn't the only Sun artist in the charts. The pop confections that Clement had written and produced for Johnny Cash, "Ballad of a Teenage Queen" and "Guess Things Happen That Way," became top-twenty hits. Phillips was the talk of the industry. The envy of the industry. He did it from his tiny storefront studio with a skeleton staff. Journalist Edwin Howard captured this moment vividly in a story for the *Memphis Press-Scimitar*. "Behind the dusty, bent Venetian blinds," he wrote, "stands the man who in six years, has brought a brand-new industry to Memphis. The office is identified only by a small neon sign in the window, which says Memphis Recording Service. The man is Sam C. Phillips. He stands because, although he has made roughly $2 million for himself in those six years, he has no desk at which to sit. 'If I have a real long telephone call, I will ask someone to get up and let me sit down.'"

But as fast as it came, it went.

In May 1958, Jerry Lee Lewis went on his first overseas tour. Six months earlier he'd snuck off to Hernando, Mississippi, to marry his thirteen-year-old cousin, Myra Gale Brown. Soon after they arrived in London, the press picked up on a chance remark from one of his entourage about Jerry's wife being rather young. Within days he was greeted with jeers at his concerts. Newspaper interviews only made things worse when he revealed that he had been a bigamist at age sixteen. Of course the news crossed the Atlantic. Phillips was devastated: "He was the hottest thing going. Jerry's innocence back then, trying to be open and friendly and engaging with press, backfired. They scalped him. So many people wanted to do in rock 'n' roll, and this was just what they were looking for. It should never have played a role of such significance in Jerry's life." Lewis said that his booking fee dropped from $10,000 a night to $250. Both numbers were probably on the high side, but he impressed all those around him with his refusal to indulge in self-pity.

Johnny Cash left in July. Columbia Records had promised him all he wanted: higher royalties, creative freedom, better sales and marketing, and perhaps some help getting Western movie roles. The attention lavished upon Jerry Lee Lewis also galled Cash, or that's what Phillips came to believe. At the time, he felt betrayed. Roy Orbison also left mid-year, and Carl Perkins had already gone.

Between Lewis's fall from grace and Cash's departure eight weeks later, Phillips bought a property just two blocks from the old studio. It had been a vending and amusement machine repair school ("For white veterans only"), a firing range, and a bakery. It was a Midas muffler

Above: Sam Phillips's assistant Marion Keisker at her desk
in the front lobby of the Memphis Recording Service.

shop when it went on the market in 1957 for $37,500. When Phillips talked to Edwin Howard, he embraced the modesty of the old studio, but soon became fired up by the potential of the new one.

Phillips's first sound engineering jobs had been for the big bands that played at the Peabody Hotel for dancing and broadcast. Nearly everything on Sun to that point had been the antithesis of the sleekness and sterility of those bands. For a time in 1956 and 1957, the world seemed to be seeing it Phillips's way. The criteria for pop airplay suddenly broadened. If a country singer could sound less country and substitute a piano and chorus for fiddle and steel guitar, he or she stood a shot at pop airplay. Jim Reeves, Sonny James, Marty Robbins, and others did just that. Some R&B singers, notably Fats Domino and Chuck Berry, approached the center from the other side. Pop records had once been made almost exclusively in New York, Los Angeles, or Chicago. Overnight, or so it seemed, they started coming from New Orleans, Phoenix, Cincinnati, Dallas, Nashville . . . and Memphis.

But then the old order began reasserting itself. Bigger groups, written arrangements, and an altogether safer sound returned. Industry-wide specs for stereo recording and playback

SUN

M-21
2:10

Instrumental

YULEVILLE, U. S. A.
THE
ROCKIN' STOCKIN'
1960

MEMPHIS, TENNESSEE

Two seasonal adjustments (and an out-of-sequence release number) to celebrate Christmas 1960. The Rockin' Stockins were Billy Riley and his band.

were agreed on in March 1958. It all meant larger studios and new hardware. The chance of playing all night to stumble onto the right song and an off-the-cuff arrangement was pretty much gone. Phillips saw the coming change, but never truly embraced it. He entrusted more of the production duties to Jack Clement and a schooled musician, Bill Justis, but dismissed them both in February 1959.

In August 1959, *Billboard*'s "On the Beat" column was devoted to Sun Records, and it began with a sober acknowledgment: "When people think of Sun Records . . . today, they are more likely to think of . . . artists who used to be with the indie Memphis label." Sun was touting Carl Mann, a lightweight singer whose goosed-up take on "Mona Lisa" was a hit that summer, and an entry into the kiddies' market with an eleven-year-old girl singing about a parakeet. The kids song was a one-off, but it underscored that Sun was losing direction.

THE OTHER LABELS

Although Sun was always Phillips's marquee label, he started two affiliates, Flip Records and Phillips International.

Flip was launched in January 1955 to test artists with more local appeal. Phillips was probably unaware that in 1951 a record distributor in Los Angeles, Max Feirtag, had started a label of the same name. Phillips's first Flip release was Carl Perkins's debut. Three more country and a few R&B releases followed before Phillips folded Flip, possibly recognizing that Feirtag had prior call. A couple of years later, Feirtag's label issued the original version of "Louie, Louie."

In 1957, at the height of Phillips's success, he launched another subsidiary, Phillips International. Feeling that Sun was typecast as a rock 'n' roll label, he wanted to explore other styles of music, but the new label's three major hits were all rock 'n' roll. Bill Justis's "Raunchy" (*see p. 189*) became one of the biggest instrumental hits of the 1950s. Carl Mann's "Mona Lisa" was issued in 1959 and Charlie Rich's "Lonely Weekends" the following year. The eight album releases were as eclectic as Phillips promised. Country gospel, supper club jazz, big band, and one now classic LP by Delta bluesman Frank Frost (*see p. 199*).

In 1963, Phillips reached a settlement with the Dutch electrical giant Philips (with one /). Philips had entered the European record business the same year that Phillips had launched his first studio. Planning an expansion into North America, the company wanted exclusive use of its name or anything similar to it. For a price, Phillips agreed.

"I just knew that this was great music. My greatest contribution was to open up an area of freedom within the artist himself, to help him to express what he believed his message to be."

— Sam Phillips

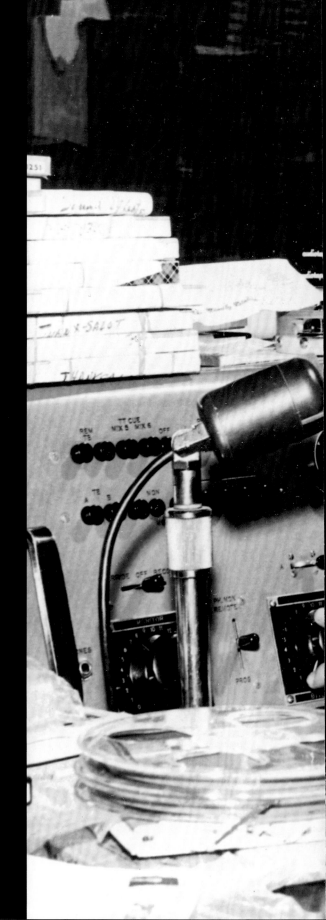

Sam Phillips at the console, April 1959, just months before the original studio was closed.

THE ONES WHO GOT AWAY

Top: The Rockhousers with Harold Jenkins (Conway Twitty) center.

Bottom: B.B. King

In a business as capricious as music, no one bats a thousand. The man who signed the Rolling Stones to Decca Records in England was the same guy who auditioned the Beatles and Brian Poole & the Tremeloes on the same day, and decided that Poole was the better bet. Lou Levy at Leeds Music had a stellar career in management and song publishing, but signed Bob Dylan as a songwriter in January 1962, only to cut him loose in July.

Signing Elvis Presley, Johnny Cash, and Jerry Lee Lewis between 1954 and 1956 is as close as anyone ever came to batting a thousand, and it secured Phillips's place among the Rock & Roll Hall of Fame's charter class of inductees. Even so, some artists slipped through his fingers. In hearing their music through the prism of what he understood and loved, he couldn't see their full potential.

Early on, before launching Sun, Phillips recorded two titans of postwar blues: B. B. King and Howlin' Wolf. King became the all-time best-selling blues musician, but his sessions were custom jobs for Modern Records' RPM label, so hanging on to him wasn't an option. Wolf, however, was Phillips's discovery. Phillips always insisted that he would have recorded him forever, but because he'd placed Wolf with Chess Records, he could do nothing when Chess enticed him to Chicago. Losing Wolf seemed to be a much bigger blow to Phillips than losing Presley.

By 1956, Sun Records had become a magnet for kids with guitars. Harold Jenkins drove from Helena, Arkansas, with a song he'd written for his band, the Rockhousers. Phillips liked Jenkins's song, "Rock House," and acquired it for his new artist, Roy Orbison. Then

Left: Roy Orbison—new label, new decade, new look.

Below: Charley Pride.

he began working with Jenkins. Years later they met again. "I know you were disappointed that we didn't release a song on you," Phillips told him, inviting him to come listen to the old tapes. Jenkins took up the offer, but was saddened to find that he sounded more characterless than he remembered. Sun was the place, but he was trying to conform to what others were doing. It took a name change to Conway Twitty and several more years before he found a style to call his own.

Orbison drove from West Texas to audition at Sun. He came with a song, "Ooby Dooby" (*see p. 148*), that was charting locally. Phillips signed him, and "Ooby Dooby" reached number fifty-nine on the Billboard Hot 100. Orbison even stayed at Phillips's house for a time. Phillips saw the particularity in Orbison's voice but couldn't see where it might go. The exquisite yearning of Orbison's pop symphonettes was beyond Phillips's field of vision. Phillips couldn't guide him there, and his studio couldn't accommodate half the musicians Orbison would have needed.

In 1958, around the time that Orbison departed Sun, a pitcher for the Memphis Red Sox, a Negro League baseball team, came in with his guitar to audition a song he'd written, "Walkin' the Stroll." Charley Pride's baseball career would soon end, but his music career wouldn't take off for another seven years. It's possible that Pride auditioned for Phillips's engineer-producer Jack Clement. If so, it's ironic that when Pride went to Nashville in 1965 with the goal of becoming country music's first Black star, the producer who latched on to his potential was Clement. Among the labels that passed on him was Mercury, then run by Shelby Singleton.

"Sam was a genius with three or four pieces," said another Sun artist, Ray Harris (*see p. 156*). "When it got beyond that . . . boom!" Harris went on to cofound Hi Records, where Al Green became a 1970s superstar. Phillips tacitly acknowledged that it wasn't his world any more by moving on to other endeavors, but for ten years his ears rarely failed him. Rarely but not invariably.

"Sam was a genius with three or four pieces."

—Ray Harris

1960 THE NEW STUDIO

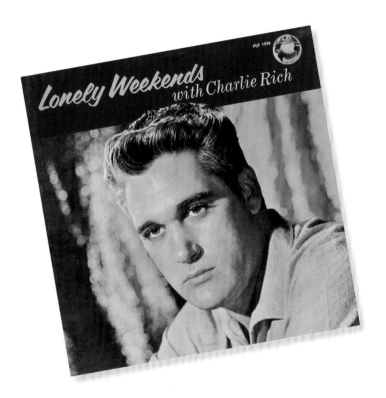

Right: Opening day at Sam Phillips Recording, September 1960.

Left: Charlie Rich's "Lonely Weekends" bridged the two studios. The bed track was recorded at the Memphis Recording Service; overdubs and reverb were added at Phillips Recording.

Aside from Jerry Lee Lewis, whose career seemed unsalvageable, the only Sun artist to touch Phillips's soul and consistently tempt him to the studio was Charlie Rich. Bill Justis had brought Rich to Sun as a songwriter, but Cash's departure and Lewis's unannounced but still very apparent blacklisting took away the potential for a songwriter's steady paycheck. Rich could play all the music Phillips loved, but needed commercial direction. His first single was recorded one month after Cash left. The third, "Lonely Weekends" (*see p. 190*), was recorded at the old studio in October 1959 and overdubbed at the new one. Released on Sun's Phillips International subsidiary in 1960, it reached number twenty-two on the Billboard chart. The following year, Jerry Lee Lewis's revival of Ray Charles's "What'd I Say" (*see p. 196*) reached number thirty. They were the last hits on Sun and its associated labels under Phillips's ownership.

Between "Lonely Weekends" and "What'd I Say," the Sam Phillips Recording Service officially opened on Madison Avenue. It's hard to know who attended the opening of the Memphis Recording Service just over ten years earlier. Probably Phillips's wife, Becky, his assistant, Marion Keisker, and possibly the Phillips's sons, Knox and Jerry. It was the culmination of Phillips's dream, but it went unremarked in the local papers and national music trade press. The Sam Phillips Recording Service, on the other hand, opened with a guest list of two hundred and a nighttime dance on the Memphis Queen II riverboat.

INSIDE THE SUN STUDIOS

In January 1956, Elvis Presley recorded his first session for RCA. In an attempt to re-create the sound of his Sun singles, RCA's engineers set up a speaker at one end of a hallway and a microphone at the other to pick up the reverberated sound. "Heartbreak Hotel" was the result. Awash in unfocused echo, it missed the target by a mile. Sam Phillips had created one of popular music's signature sounds. Replicating it was not so easy, even for the best engineers in the business. Columbia Records found the same thing when they signed Johnny Cash in 1958. It wasn't enough to slather echo onto a song. That wasn't the secret.

Phillips opened his Memphis Recording Service in January 1950, less than two years after the first commercial tape recorder was introduced. The Ampex Electric and Manufacturing Company had adapted some equipment captured from the German military during the last days of World War II. Its first recorder cost $7,500, and even when the price dropped to $5,200 (roughly $60,000 today), it was still impossibly far out of Phillips's reach. Introduced in April 1953, Ampex's Model 350 sold for less than $1,000, and Phillips scrimped and saved until he could afford one. Soon afterward, he bought another. Two tape recorders made his sound possible.

Phillips's background was engineering live radio shows. He'd taken a few courses in circuitry during World War II, but he'd learned on the job how to optimize microphone placement and room acoustics. After he bought the second Ampex tape recorder, he took the signals from the four microphones on his studio floor and bounced them between the console and the two recorders. This tightly focused tape-delay *slapback* echo was very unlike chamber echo. The easiest way to think of it is as a single adjustable repetition, instead of the multiple diminishing repetitions you'd hear yelling down from the rim of a canyon. It was the difference between *presence* and *distance* and created a very full sound from few instruments. On Jerry Lee Lewis's "Whole Lot of Shakin' Going On," the piano feeds back upon itself so that the record throbs with life before the drums come in or Lewis starts singing.

The original Memphis Recording Service studio floor measured just eighteen by thirty-three feet. Cramped even by the standards of the time. After stereo recording became the industry norm, small studios became impracticable because the instruments and vocalists couldn't be physically separated. With that in mind, Phillips bought a property two blocks away and began constructing a new studio.

The official opening of the Sam Phillips Recording Service was on September 17, 1960. Four times the size of the old studio, Sam Phillips Recording had movable baffles for stereo separation, a recreation room for musicians, offices, a tape storage room, mastering room, executive bar, and a rooftop lounge. The décor was space-age midcentury modern. The dominant color was teal. For some reason, Phillips eschewed slapback for chamber echo. It took some years before the new studio sounded as intimate as the old one.

Sam Phillips's two Memphis studios are still there. Sam Phillips Recording has been open since 1960, looking much as it always did inside and out. For most of 1960 the old studio was unoccupied. Piles of records, correspondence, invoices, lunch tabs from Taylor's Restaurant next door, and bits and pieces of furniture littered the floor. By December, it had been cleared out and the landlord had rented it to the Underwater Sport Shop. Several other tenants followed until it reopened as a tourist attraction in 1979. Later, it once again became a functioning studio, operating after the last tourist had left for the day. On July 31, 2003, one day after Phillips's death, the original site of the Memphis Recording Service on Union Avenue was designated as a National Historic Landmark.

Above: Sam Phillips's dyed his hair blonde on the occasion of the new studio's opening. Here, he sits in his office atop the complex. September 1960. That's a personal jukebox to his left.

Opposite: Sam Phillips's A&R man Charles Underwood prepares to call for a "take" at Sam Phillips Recording, September 1960.

1968

"WOOLY BULLY" AND THE LAST SINGLE

Right: Sam Phillips Recording today.

Opposite: Sam the Sham (center) with a pyramid of Pharoahs on South Highland Street, Memphis, 1965.

When Phillips relaunched Sun in 1953, he had competition from two new local labels: Lester Bihari's Meteor Records and Duke Records, started by James Mattis and Bill Fitzgerald. Meteor sputtered along for four more years, and Duke was soon acquired by the company in Houston that had sued Phillips over his first hit, "Bear Cat" (*see p. 75*). In the early 1960s, though, Sun was eclipsed by local competition from Stax and Hi Records, both of them finely attuned to the local R&B scene in a way that Phillips once was. They built studios with second-hand equipment, duct tape, trial-and-error acoustics, and a blazing quest to succeed, just as Phillips had. They broadened the appeal of from-the-roots Black music, as Phillips had.

Jerry Lee Lewis and Charlie Rich left Sun in 1963. Phillips had moved on to other ventures—properties with mineral rights, radio stations, and so on. In his mind, he'd left the record business. He and his A&R men didn't cultivate contacts in the Black community who could have brought the region's new R&B singers to the label; neither did they infiltrate the city's underground scene. Knox Phillips wanted to chase it all, but his father was unwilling to commit the funds. Sam Phillips Recording didn't even become the first call for out-of-town labels looking for the Memphis pixie dust. That call went to American Sound Studio, two miles north on Thomas Street. That's where B. J. Thomas, Dusty Springfield, and even Elvis Presley went. The only major hit recorded at Sam Phillips's studio in the '60s was Sam the Sham and the Pharaohs' "Wooly Bully" in 1964. Producer Stan Kesler, who'd played on many Sun sessions and written two of Presley's Sun recordings, leased "Wooly Bully" to MGM Records.

The last single on Sam Phillips's original Sun Records appeared in January 1968. It was a remake of the Supremes' "Back in My Arms Again" by a local frat party band, Load of Mischief. It wasn't announced as the last record. There just wasn't another one.

THE 70 RECORDINGS
BY PETER GURALNICK

A WORD ABOUT THE SELECTION OF THE 70

I feel as if I need to explain myself. I wrote this as a kind of narrative, not just to introduce you to some of Sun and Sam Phillips' greatest music, but also to try to tell a little bit of the story of Sam Phillips and Sun Records through the music.

So it's not, strictly speaking, a "Best Of" selection—though there are certainly many, probably most, that would qualify for any "Best Of" list. Some of the tracks are designed to help tell the story, to chart the progression of Sun, and the evolution of Sam Phillips's creative thinking, over the ten years that mark the pinnacle of his record-making career, a decade in which, as legendary Atlantic Records head Jerry Wexler once said, "he produced a millennium's worth of music."

One further note of clarification: The first four records on my list are not Sun records. They are Sam records, all but one of them recorded by Sam in 1951 and released on the Chess and RPM labels (the fourth, Joe Hill Louis's "Gotta Let You Go," was released on Sam's eponymous, one-shot "It's the Phillips" label), and they are here because they lay the groundwork for the birth of Sun Records—and rock 'n' roll.

The one thing that comes across most strikingly when you listen to the records (and I hope you listen to them all, and all the recordings they will lead to) is how ferociously Sam believed in the music. It would change the world, he said unblinkingly, starting with his very first interviews, in 1951, about Jackie Brenston and Ike Turner's "Rocket '88'." And I think I need hardly add: He was right.

Sam Phillips had lots of sayings, many of which stick with me to this day. One of my favorites is, "Hell, if you're not having fun, it isn't worth doing." That's something I've pondered many times. But I can assure you (and Sam), putting together this list, trying to give a sense of the story line, most of all writing about the music in as close as I can come to the celebratory spirit in which it was recorded, has been a ball.

Left: Ike Turner (with guitar) leading the Kings of Rhythm. Jackie Brenston is top left with saxophone. c. 1956.

Previous spread: Roy Orbison in the recording studio.

PRELUDE TO A REVOLUTION

Rosco Gordon heading up his self-titled orchestra, with Billy "Red" Love on the piano.

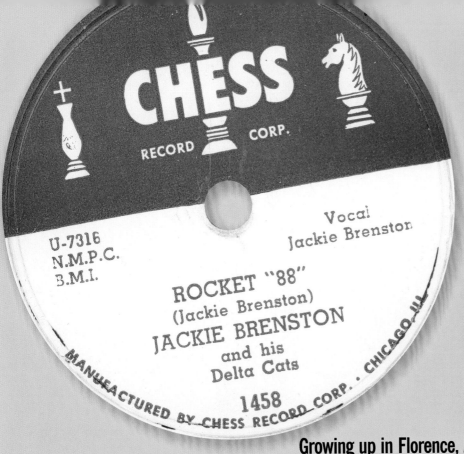

ROCKET "88"
Jackie Brenston and His Delta Cats

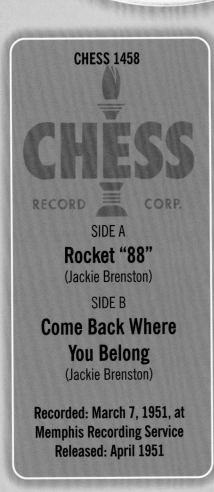

CHESS 1458

SIDE A
Rocket "88"
(Jackie Brenston)

SIDE B
Come Back Where You Belong
(Jackie Brenston)

Recorded: March 7, 1951, at Memphis Recording Service
Released: April 1951

Left: Jackie Brenston.

Inset: Brenston's "Rocket 88" is blasting off, in this early print ad.

Growing up in Florence, Alabama, where he was born in 1923, Sam Phillips said he heard everything. "Nothing passed my ears. A mockingbird or a whippoorwill—out in the country on a calm afternoon. The silence of the cottonfields, that beautiful rhythmic silence, with a hoe hitting a rock every now and then and just as it spaded through the dirt, you could hear it." But most of all he could be said to have heard the sound of America singing, as he worked beside Black families in the fields on the 323-acre farm that his father rented.

The course of his life was forever set when at sixteen he and his brother and some of their friends drove down Beale Street (frequently celebrated as "Black America's Main Street") in the early hours before dawn, on their way to a prayer meeting in Dallas. "Well, I'd heard about Beale Street all my life, pictured it in my mind what it was—I could not wait! We arrived at four or five o'clock in the morning in pouring-down rain, but I'm telling you, Broadway never looked that busy. It was like a beehive, a microcosm of humanity. . . . But the most impressive thing to me about Beale Street was that nobody got in anybody's way—because every damn one of them wanted to be right there."

That was why he took a job with a Memphis radio station in 1945, and that was why he opened a studio, which he called the Memphis Recording Service ("I wanted it to sound big—I was so little, and Memphis, boy, I mean, Memphis, Tennessee, was bigger than the world") in a small walk-in storefront on January 1, 1950. It was with the intention, as he often said, of offering an opportunity to "some of those great Negro artists in the South [who] just had no place to go."

"With the belief that I had in this music, in these people," he would say on later occasions, "I would have been the biggest damn coward on God's green earth if I had not opened [those] doors."

It was the dawning of a new era.

It was difficult to find people to record at first—and he was barely able to keep his little studio afloat with the commercial work that he took on, including funerals, bar mitzvahs, talent contests, and "personal" acetates for people who just walked in off the street wanting to hear the sound of their own voice. His first success came some fourteen months after opening up when a nineteen-year-old from Clarksdale, Mississippi, arrived with his band, the Kings of Rhythm.

Ike Turner had heard about Sam from Riley King, a local star on Memphis's WDIA, the first all-Black radio station in the country, universally hailed as "the Mother Station of the Negroes." King

FIRST TIME IN MEMPHIS!
W.C. HANDY THEATRE
2 DAYS ONLY - SAT. & SUN. APRIL 7 - 8
ON STAGE! ----- IN PERSON

★ **JACKIE BRENSTON** ★

THE TERRIFIC **ROCKET "88"** SENSATION

★ WITH ★

IKE TURNER

"THE KING OF THE PIANO"
AND
★ — **"HIS KING OF RHYTHM"** — ★

JACKIE IS GONNA TEAR THE HOUSE DOWN

ADMISSION _____ 60¢ ax. Incl.

Right: The car that was the inspiration for the song: the Oldsmobile Super 88.

Left: Handbill from the Handy Theatre featuring Jackie and Ike, April 1951.

"With the belief that I had in this music, in these people, I would have been the biggest damn coward on God's green earth if I had not opened [those] doors."

—Sam Phillips

had soon become known there as B. B. King, which could variously stand for "Blues Boy" "The Singing Black Boy," or "The Boy from Beale Street." He had already cut several records in the studio for the Los Angeles–based RPM label without a great deal of success. (Sam Phillips at this point had no interest in starting his own label—he simply wanted to record the music, then license it to any label that might be interested, without any of the headaches of starting up a business in a commercial field he knew nothing about.)

The band had some trouble finding the studio. They had the address, and they had directions, but they drove right past it several times because, with its neon-lit sign, it looked more like a barber shop to them than anything else. When they walked in and unloaded their instruments, they immediately recognized that they had a problem. Their three-hour journey to Memphis had been interrupted several times by police stops (for "driving while Black") and flat tires, and on one of those stops they had damaged the guitar amp. When the incongruously dapper young White man plugged it in and turned on the power, there was a loud buzzing noise, and after examining it Sam Phillips pronounced that they had a busted speaker cone. Ike Turner was beside himself. Was there some place nearby they could rent an amplifier? But Sam Phillips seemed strangely undaunted. He *liked* the sound, he said, it was original, it was *different*—which for him evidently was the hallmark of creativity.

And so they cut the record, with baritone saxophonist Jackie Brenston taking the vocals (and improbably enough getting his name on the record when it came out) and the buzz from the speaker providing an undercurrent that Phillips said gave the record not only a unique sound (it was the "rubbing" between the saxophone and the distorted guitar that captured Sam's attention from the start) but an unstoppable rhythmic pulse.

When the record was released on the Chess label just three weeks later, it was a hit beyond anyone's imagining. Within two months, it was number 1 on the R&B charts, and before long it had sold more than one hundred thousand copies. It was in one sense a helluva start in the record business. But to Sam Phillips it was something else. When the band appeared at the W. C. Handy Theatre in Memphis's Orange Mound neighborhood, he somehow inveigled a reporter from the *Memphis Commercial Appeal* to come out and write about them. It was a great opportunity to advertise himself and his studio—but more than that, it served as a platform for the unequivocal belief at the heart of his whole recording scheme. As he had declared in an earlier story in the paper trumpeting the record's success, he was "convinced the Rocket will move out of the race field into general popularity." That was the vision that propelled him, that was Sam Phillips's articulated vision of the future: that this music would break down barriers, musical, social, above all racial. And that was something in which he would firmly believe all his life.

SHE'S DYNAMITE
B. B. King

RPM 323

SIDE A
She's Dynamite
(Tampa Red)

SIDE B
B. B. Blues
(King–Taub)

Recorded: May 27, 1951 (Side A) and January 28, 1951 (Side B), at Memphis Recording Service
Released: Summer 1951

Left: B. B. King back when "Lucille" was a Telecaster.

Sam set out to further this vision immediately with B. B. King, the young radio star who had sent Turner to him. All of B. B.'s recordings to date had been conventional enough, what Sam would term "polite" blues, modeled on popular recordings of the day. The owners of the RPM label, the Bihari brothers in Los Angeles, had sent Sam a new release by Tampa Red, one of the most popular blues recording stars of the '30s and '40s, with the idea that B. B. would cover it. But Sam had something altogether different in mind. With a band put together by local bandleader Phineas Newborn Sr., which consisted primarily of himself on drums and his sons Phineas Jr. on piano and sixteen-year-old Calvin on guitar, the song would have taken on an altogether different feel in any case, but then Sam (and Calvin Newborn's blazing lead guitar) gave it the "Rocket '88'" treatment and twenty-five-year-old B. B. King gave it a ride that he had never captured before and would never really return to again. You can hear him shouting behind the sax solo, then driving home the lyric of the final verse with a rhythmic accentuation ("You can whip it / Whop it / Hang it on the wall / Throw it out the window / She'll pitch herself a ball") before launching into the chorus one more time with a satisfied, but by no means quiescent, "Yeahhhh."

The record didn't sell, and in some ways it reveals something about Sam's unrealistic expectations. I think he really believed for a minute that he had found the formula for the breakthrough he knew was coming (and indeed he would repeat this approach one or two more times with notable aesthetic, but little commercial, success), when he had in fact only found the key to a vehicle he was yet to discover. As for B. B. King, he would find his own, very different and distinctively "pleading" voice a few months later when, after a business dispute with Sam, the Biharis took their artist back and recorded him themselves at Memphis's "colored" YMCA, and with Ike Turner on piano cut his first, unforgettable national hit, "Three O'Clock Blues," which went to number 1 on the national R&B charts in early 1952.

MOANIN' AT MIDNIGHT/HOW MANY MORE YEARS
Howlin' Wolf

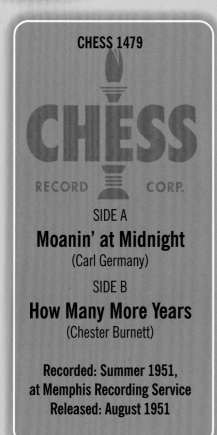

CHESS 1479

CHESS
RECORD CORP.

SIDE A
Moanin' at Midnight
(Carl Germany)

SIDE B
How Many More Years
(Chester Burnett)

Recorded: Summer 1951,
at Memphis Recording Service
Released: August 1951

Left: Howlin' Wolf at a grocery store opening, West Memphis, c. 1953.

Here we see yet another side of Sam, indivisible from his vision of an undivided America. What he loved most of all, the kind of music he had been drawn to from the first and would always come back to, was the low-down, "gutbucket" blues, the blues he had heard in the fields of Florence, the blues he heard coming from Beale Street. There was nothing, Sam felt, that could "tell the truth like the blues, something so absolutely true, so close to life" that it just cut to the core of human experience. With the Howlin' Wolf (born Chester Arthur Burnett in White Station, Mississippi, in 1910), he found the very embodiment of that truth.

He first heard Howlin' Wolf on the radio, coming in on the "worst pick-up you ever heard" from West Memphis, at almost exactly the same time that "Rocket '88'" was released. Even listening on that tinny connection, "I heard one number, and I instantly, I *instantly* said, 'THIS IS WHAT I'M LOOKING FOR.'" And when, after a period of quiet courtship ("I didn't want to overpromise anything"), he was finally able to get Wolf into the studio, "My God," he declared, "this is where the soul of man never dies."

"Moanin' at Midnight" and "How Many More Years" were the result of months of work—patient, painstaking work that was necessary, Sam was convinced, for Wolf and his band, led by Willie Johnson, a guitarist who was forging a fierce new path in the blues, to become comfortable enough in the studio to find the sound *behind* the sound that they were seeking to express. Of Wolf's scoured voice, he said it was at one and the same time both the worst voice he had ever heard in his life and, in its own inimitable way, the most beautiful. "When he opened up his mouth to sing, this guy hypnotized himself along with you. To see him on a session, it was just the greatest show—the fervor in that man's face, setting up on the front of his chair and locked into telling you individually about his trials and tribulations. He's the only artist I ever recorded that I wish I could have had a camera on—the vitality of that man was something else."

Some seventy years later, these two songs would remain among the most pure and unadulterated sounds ever captured in a recording studio. For "How Many More Years" Sam added a piano, which he felt would give the song more of a "structure." But "Moanin' at Midnight," one of the first of Sam's many poetic titles, was just pure unadulterated—well, to Sam there would have been no other way to say it: Wolf just sang "with his damn soul." When he sent influential WLAC DJ Gene Nobles a copy of the record, he wrote, "'Moanin' at Midnight' is the side. I know I'm partial, but it is the most different record I ever heard."

As it turned out, the record was a two-sided hit, with "Moanin' at Midnight" going to number 10 and "How Many More Years" going to number 4—but still it didn't fully live up to the dimensions of Sam's faith in Wolf, who would go on to enjoy a long and illustrious (and uncompromising and undiminished) career on Chess Records, where he and Muddy Waters would rule the world of modern Chicago blues. Wolf, Sam always believed (though I must confess I never quite grasped how it could have been done) could have been "the counterpart of Elvis—this guy would have been huge with White youngsters, along with Black." He would have provided, Sam said, an "entirely different approach to rock 'n' roll."

IT'S THE

pHILLIps

"HOTTEST THING IN THE COUNTRY"

One Man Band   Vocal—Louis

(Louis - Phillips)
JOE HILL LOUIS
GOTTA LET YOU GO

9001

IT'S THE

pHILLIps

(HOTTEST THING IN THE COUNTRY)
9001, 9002

SIDE A
Gotta Let You Go
(Louis—Phillips)

SIDE B
Boogie in the Park
(Louis—Phillips)

Recorded: July 1950 at Memphis
Recording Service
Released: August 21, 1950

Right: Joe Hill Louis.

GOTTA LET YOU GO
Joe Hill Louis

Almost from the beginning Sam was confounded by the business of the record "business." Within days of recording B. B. King for the first time in the summer of 1950, he fell into a bitter dispute with the Bihari brothers over the matter of a royalties arrangement that he felt he had been promised and the Biharis emphatically said he had not. His immediate response, despite the fact that all of his better instincts told him not to, was to start his own label. So in August of 1950, well before the success of "Rocket '88'," that is just what he did, in partnership with charismatic DJ Dewey Phillips, whose *Red Hot and Blue* show on mainstream radio station WHBQ had a passionate following among Black and White listeners alike.

From the time they first met, Sam and Dewey considered themselves brothers, a confusion only furthered by the conjunction of their names. Joe Hill Louis was the first artist to wander into the Memphis Recording Service in the first month or two after its opening, and he subsequently brought many of his friends. It was only natural, then, that Sam should inaugurate his new label, called, appropriately enough, It's the Phillips, with Louis, and that the record should reflect as raw and gut-bucket (not to mention chaotic) a feel as any record that Sam would ever release. Modeled on John Lee Hooker's 1949 best-seller, "Boogie Chillen," a landmark of the downhome blues movement and one of Sam's chief points of reference over the years (with its driving beat, it may well have been the downhome blues' first and only million seller), "Gotta Let You Go" tells an exuberantly garbled tale leading into a chorus that frequently comes as a relief.

Joe Hill Louis (real name Leslie Hill—the first and last names were appropriated from the legendary heavyweight boxing champion) recorded many more times over the years for Sam, and often in better tune, but none of his efforts represented the spirit of the age better than this one. Unfortunately "Gotta Let You Go"/"Boogie in the Park" was the one and only release on the It's the Phillips label, as Sam soon discovered that business was not exactly Dewey's forte, though they remained brothers to the end.

DRIVIN' SLOW
Johnny London
(Alto Wizard)

Right: Johnny London—Alto Wizard.

Previous spread: Elvis Presley.

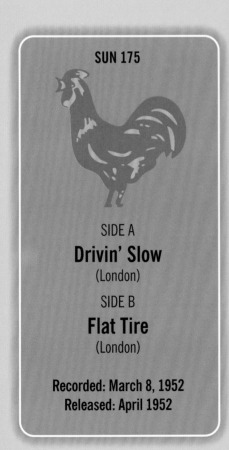

SUN 175

SIDE A
Drivin' Slow
(London)

SIDE B
Flat Tire
(London)

Recorded: March 8, 1952
Released: April 1952

The Sun label's first official release, in April 1952. Johnny London was fifteen years old, a sophomore at Melrose High School, and an obvious admirer of popular rhythm-and-blues saxophonist Earl Bostic, when he wandered into the studio (he and his little combo just "wanted to record," he said). This slow-drag R&B instrumental was a far cry from the music that Sam had declared to be his mission but, as Johnny recalled, Sam just "fell in love with what we were doing, and he decided that he'd 'hire' us." Initially Sam recorded two sides, one with a vocal by his wife Becky, a captivating radio announcer with a fine pop voice, but a week later he called the band back in and recorded the B side that would make up their one release on the newly formed, and newly named, Sun label.

To Sam, the name seemed almost obvious. "I wanted something short, simple, [with] a common denominator that was hard to forget." It's hard to say what exactly he heard in the combo's sound. The B side, "Flat Tire," was little more than a novelty number with an oddly distorted sound. On "Drivin' Slow" the sound is no less odd. Johnny plays a harsh, almost distorted alto lead, while the tenor repeats a bluesy riff in the background and the piano supplies steady support. According to Johnny, Sam made them do the number over and over until "he found the sound that he wanted," a "hollow sound" that, Johnny was certain, he had never tried before. "He created a chamber that he didn't have, something similar to a telephone booth. It was a home-made thing, 8' by 4', something like that."

The real question is why. One way to look at it, I suppose, is as a "sonic experiment" intended to provide an unorthodox dip into commercial R&B waters. In any case, I never knew Sam to address the question except to say, "As an instrumental number it would be more difficult to sell." It didn't and, out of money and discouraged by the utter lack of success of his first three releases, Sam shut down the label within two months of its start.

SEEMS LIKE A MILLION YEARS

Willie Nix

When Sam started up Sun again in January 1953, Willie Nix's "Seems Like a Million Years," another in Nix's string of arrestingly declarative downhome sides, was in the first batch of releases. Willie Nix was a drummer, and a great eccentric, who was described by a fellow bluesman as "a little aviatic" in his thinking, something that would have immediately recommended him to Sam. He had originally come to Sam's attention at the same time that he first heard Howlin' Wolf, and in the same manner, through his broadcasts on West Memphis radio station KWEM.

By 1953 Sam had already recorded a number of sessions on him and put out releases on both Chess and RPM, but his one Sun release was certainly among his best. As Sam said, "Willie was not the subtlest of drummers, but he drove a session along," and here, with seventeen-year-old James Cotton on harmonica and Willie Johnson stand-in Joe Willie Wilkins on guitar, he was able to suggest a convincingly fatalistic message without ever forfeiting his sense of forward motion, however *ritardano* it might be musically expressed. "Some drinks to keep from worrying," Nix declared, "Some just ride from town to town / No need for me to drink to keep from worrying / 'Cause it's slowly carrying me down." But the little combo never let up, and the lyrics of the song never dragged down its mood of almost cheerful acceptance of the way things were and, apparently, had to be.

Left: Willie with Joe Willie Wilkins on guitar.

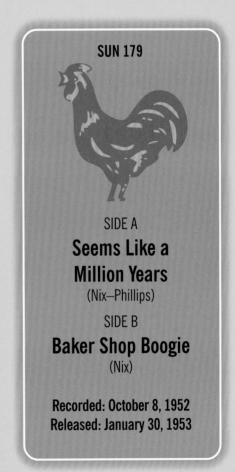

SUN 179

SIDE A
Seems Like a Million Years
(Nix–Phillips)

SIDE B
Baker Shop Boogie
(Nix)

Recorded: October 8, 1952
Released: January 30, 1953

EASY/ BEFORE LONG
Jimmy and Walter

SUN 180

SIDE A
Easy
SIDE B
Before Long
(DeBerry)

Recorded: February 25, 1953
Released: March 1953

"Easy" represents a pinnacle of blues recording. The 1950s were the decade of the blues harmonica, led by the brilliant improvisational skills of Little Walter (Jacobs), who started out as a sideman in Muddy Waters's band and went on to surpass his mentor in commercial success. Walter Horton, variously known as Big Walter, Shakey Walter, and "Mumbles," was almost ten years older than Little Walter and one of the earliest artists recorded by Sam, with his first release on the Biharis' Modern label appearing well before "Juke," Little Walter's breakthrough instrumental hit.

Never the kind of harmonic improviser that the younger man proved to be, Horton throughout his career focused primarily on *sound*—and that's what you have here, every variation that can be gotten out of a blues harmonica, from a whisper to an all-out auditory assault, as he creates sonic waves off the melody of Ivory Joe Hunter's massive blues hit, "I Almost Lost My Mind," while Jimmy DeBerry provides inconspicuous accompaniment on guitar. This is the kind of music that can be listened to without interruption again and again— you'll never get tired of it. And it might be noted that the other side, DeBerry's "Before Long," on which Walter does not play at all, was described by Sam's indispensable assistant and office manager, Marion Keisker (the only other person working at Sun during its first four years of existence), as an almost perfect example of the "beautiful simplicity" that Sam was always looking for, achieved only with great (but determinedly unobservable) effort.

*Right: Walter Horton in England
for the 1965 Folk Blues Festival.*

"Too Dig-a-Gow!"
Rufus Thomas, Jr.

WDIA
50,000 Watts of Goodwill

BEAR CAT (The Answer to "Hound Dog") Rufus "Hound Dog" Thomas Jr.

Sun's first hit, and an occasion for both great celebration and a considerable amount of financial disappointment. It was, as the title proclaims, an "answer song," in this case to Big Mama Thornton's phenomenally successful "Hound Dog," which, of course, would be recorded three years later in a very different version by a twenty-one-year-old Elvis Presley. Just to emphasize how closely the two songs were linked, "Bear Cat," by WDIA DJ Rufus Thomas, came out the same week that the original "Hound Dog" first charted. Rufus's version is full of raucous good cheer, as nearly all of his subsequent releases would be (Rufus, after all, was the man who years later originated the "Funky Chicken"), but unfortunately for Sam the concept of "intellectual property" was just about to rear its head.

Rhythm and blues answer songs up to this time had generally been treated as original compositions, with songwriter credit going to the author of the response number. It was with some surprise, then, that Sam received a letter from Don Robey, the notoriously tough owner of Big Mama Thornton's label, Duke/Peacock Records, demanding that Sam recognize Robey's copyright on the material and turn over all songwriting and publishing proceeds forthwith. Sam contested the claim, lost, and ended up having to pay a substantial penalty. So "Bear Cat," for all its uninhibited exuberance, ended up losing money for the label while at the same time rising to number 3 on the R&B charts and giving Sun its first Top 10 R&B hit. Sam always insisted that it *was* original in one way at least: its title phrase, which Sam had contributed. Rufus had initially balked at recording a song that made no sense to him at first. Just what, he asked, was a "bear cat" when it came to male-female relations? Sam said he wasn't sure about Memphis, but this was a common phrase in the part of Alabama that he came from. "I said, 'Rufus, hell, you don't know what a damn bear cat is?'" And he went on to explain that in Florence, Alabama, that was how you referred to a "bossy" woman. And then Rufus gave it his all.

Left: Rufus Thomas on-air, WDIA.

SUN 181

SIDE A
Bear Cat
(Phillips)

SIDE B
Walkin' in the Rain
(Thomas, Jr.)

Recorded: March 8, 1953
Released: March 1953

LONESOME OLD JAIL
D. A. Hunt

Probably the two commercial downhome blues artists that Sam was drawn to most were John Lee Hooker and Sam "Lightnin'" Hopkins. He may have revered Hooker most of all for his rhythm, but he revered both for their flat, unadorned, wry view of the world. Here he found his Lightnin' Hopkins in D. A. Hunt, a blues singer from Anniston, Alabama, otherwise unknown, who delivers a moving blues of his own while channeling Hopkins's sound and providing echoes of some of his best-known songs, including "Hello Central," "Jailhouse Blues," and "Unsuccessful Blues."

Left: D. A. Hunt, early 1950s.

SUN 183

SIDE A
Lonesome Old Jail
(Hunt)
SIDE B
Greyhound Blues
(Hunt)

Recorded: March 11, 1953
Released: June 1953

CALL ME ANYTHING, BUT CALL ME

Big Memphis Ma Rainey

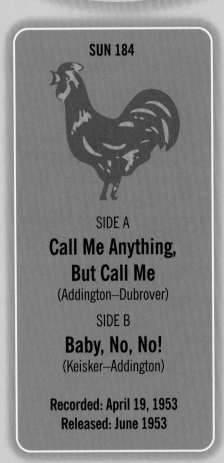

SUN 184

SIDE A
Call Me Anything, But Call Me
(Addington–Dubrover)

SIDE B
Baby, No, No!
(Keisker–Addington)

Recorded: April 19, 1953
Released: June 1953

Perhaps because of the commercial limitations of the blues market at that time, perhaps because of his own limitations (though Sam went on to proudly introduce the first "all-girl radio station in the nation," in recognition, he said, of the talent, drive, and ambition of yet another unheralded segment of the population), Sam recorded very few women, and not always with the best results. Here he introduces Big Memphis Ma Rainey (real name Lillie Mae Glover), a perennial presence on the Memphis blues scene, who falls somewhere between the classic blues mode of Bessie Smith and Glover's namesake, the original Ma Rainey (the subject of August Wilson's play *Ma Rainey's Black Bottom*) and the more strident contemporary approach of Big Mama Thornton. Maybe this was Sam's attempt to claim the Big Mama market without appropriating her song, but neither the song nor its presentation, which mixed elements of small-band R&B with vibes and the sizzling guitar of Pat Hare, another of Howlin' Wolf guitarist Willie Johnson's disciples, is particularly distinguished. On the other hand, Big Memphis Ma Rainey's unbounded enthusiasm, her vocal squalls, and her vaudevillian good humor (much like Rufus Thomas's) all come through, and perhaps give a hint of things that might have been.

Right: Big Memphis Ma Rainey (Lillie Mae Glover) showing out with Frankie Lymon.

TIME HAS MADE A CHANGE
Jimmy DeBerry

Listen for the telephone ringing. Now listen to Sam explain it. "I love perfect imperfection, I really do, and that's not just some cute saying, that's a fact. Perfect? That's the devil. Who in this world would want to be perfect? They should strike the damn thing out of the language of the human race. You think I was going to throw that cut away for one of them good ones that didn't have a telephone ringing in the middle of it? Hell, no, that's what [was] happening. That was *real*." And the telephone isn't even the weirdest thing about the record. "Time Has Made a Change" represents Jimmy DeBerry's second appearance here, this time without Walter Horton, in the summer of 1953. The whole thing is a *mess*. But at the same time, as Sam might say, "It's different, isn't it? it's a *beautiful* mess." And the difference comes across in a way that's impossible to label, certainly, but for me is equally impossible to resist.

Left: Jimmy DeBerry in the 1960s.

SUN 185

SIDE A
**Time Has Made
a Change**
(DeBerry–Burns)

SIDE B
Take a Little Chance
(DeBerry–Burns)

Recorded: May 16, 1953
Released: June 1953

**JUST WALKIN'
IN THE RAIN**
The Prisonaires

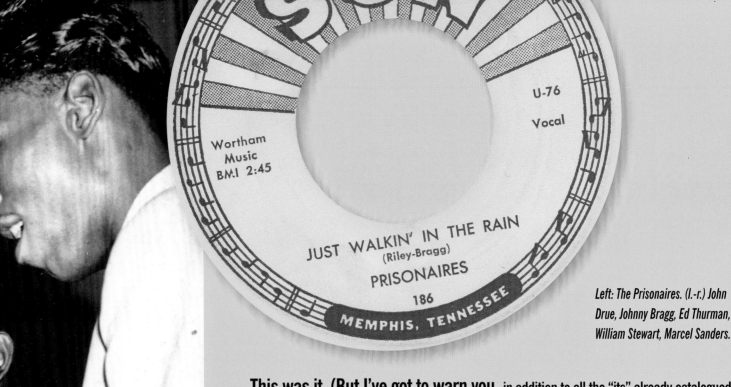

U-76
Vocal

Wortham
Music
BM.I 2:45

JUST WALKIN' IN THE RAIN
(Riley–Bragg)
PRISONAIRES
186
MEMPHIS, TENNESSEE

Left: The Prisonaires. (l.-r.) John Drue, Johnny Bragg, Ed Thurman, William Stewart, Marcel Sanders.

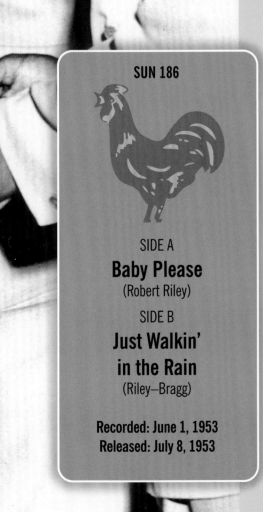

SUN 186

SIDE A
Baby Please
(Robert Riley)

SIDE B
**Just Walkin'
in the Rain**
(Riley–Bragg)

Recorded: June 1, 1953
Released: July 8, 1953

This was it. (But I've got to warn you, in addition to all the "its" already catalogued, there are still plenty more to come.) A *Life* magazine photo shoot. A Top 10 record. More than thirty thousand sales. But the story is the real grabber.

Through his short-lived partner in the new Sun label, Jim Bulleit, a wily veteran of the music business (they would break up within months), Sam had learned of a quintet that had been formed in the Tennessee State Prison in Nashville and, through the enlightened policies of the new warden and Tennessee Governor Frank Clement, was making appearances on Nashville radio and at Nashville civic functions. When he heard them, Sam said, "The devastation came over me. For something like this to come along, for all of the circumstances to be [right]—you can imagine how I thought I was dreaming!"

After bringing all of his diplomatic and oratorical skills to bear on Governor Clement (*see Howard Seratt's "Troublesome Waters," p. 98*), Sam got permission to record them not on-location at the prison but in Memphis, where he arranged for them to be transported to his "little laboratory of sound" with an armed guard on June 1, 1953. They spent the entire day recording, mostly concentrating on "Just Walkin' in the Rain," the group's signature song, as recounted by an on-the-scene *Memphis Press-Scimitar* reporter, whose story would be published a month later. This was probably the first time that eighteen-year-old Elvis Presley, just graduated from high school, heard of the studio and its adventurous young owner, "painstaking Mr. Phillips," as the newspaper article described him, who had insisted that the Prisonaires keep going "until the records were cut just right."

In the end Sam got just what he wanted, with lead singer Johnny Bragg's ethereal falsetto reminiscent of the Ink Spots' Bill Kenny, but better in a way, Sam thought, both because of the deeply emotional message embedded in its lyrics and the slight flaw in what Sam called Bragg's "tongue-tied" delivery, the imperfection that set off the perfection of the whole. He rush-released the single, and they quickly got to thirty thousand sales, but despite the efforts of Sam and his brother Jud, a master salesman associated with the company just as briefly as Jim Bulleit, they could never get past that initial sales mark, and in the end it broke up Sam's partnership with Bulleit. But he had at least created a record that, both in its furtherance of a social cause in which he deeply believed and in the sheer beauty of its setting, would stand forever and uniquely apart from any other record in the Sam Phillips catalogue. On the other hand, with that said, how many others of Sam's records could legitimately make a similar claim?

FEELIN' GOOD
LITTLE JUNIOR'S
BLUE FLAMES
187
MEMPHIS, TENNESSEE

FEELIN' GOOD
Little Junior's Blue Flames

Right: Junior Parker.

SUN 187

SIDE A
Feelin' Good
(Parker)

SIDE B
Fussin' and Fightin' Blues
(Parker)

Recorded: June 18, 1953
Released: July 1953

This would have to be considered the purest and most unadulterated take-off on John Lee Hooker's "Boogie Chillen" in the Sun catalogue, and it was recorded by a young, smooth-voiced harmonica player from West Memphis (though there is no harmonica here), who would have preferred to be recording a jump blues along the lines of plummy singers like Roy Brown. Just listen to the first "Wellllllll . . ." if you want to be convinced of Sam's persuasive powers. ("I just had him hold that [note]. I mean, he held it a little while, but that wasn't enough. I wanted to hear 'Wellllllll' as long as he could hold it—and just boogie behind.") Just listen to the unambiguous verve and enthusiasm that Little Junior Parker summons up. And most of all, listen to the driving rhythms of the Blue Flames—the unrelenting, unstoppable rhythm that was the hallmark of almost everything that Sam sought in a record (not the Prisonaires) as well as an unmistakable harbinger of what would soon come to be called "rock 'n' roll." Over the years Sam would come back to this same theme many times, most notably with the "Sammy Lewis-Willie Johnson Combo" (*see p. 126*) and a fine version by Jerry Lee Lewis entitled (for the age in which it was created) "I've Been Twistin'." But it was Little Junior Parker who took the prize with what turned out to be Sam's third Top 10 R&B hit in the summer and fall of 1953.

"*I love perfect imperfection, I really do. Perfect? That's the devil. There's too much powder and rouge around. People want the real thing.*"

—Sam Phillips

TIGER MAN
(King of the Jungle)
Rufus Thomas, Jr.

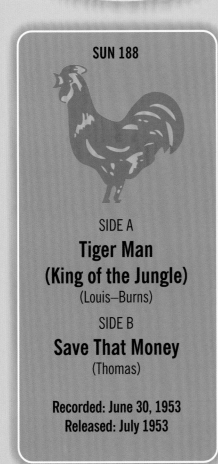

SUN 188

SIDE A

**Tiger Man
(King of the Jungle)**
(Louis–Burns)

SIDE B

Save That Money
(Thomas)

Recorded: June 30, 1953
Released: July 1953

Left: Rufus selling it in the recording studio.

*Previous page: Sun recording artists Dusty
Brooks and the Sepia Tones, c. 1953.*

The return of the Blue Flames, most of them anyway, two weeks after recording "Feelin' Good" (*see p. 84*), led by eighteen-year-old Floyd Murphy (younger brother of future Blues Brother Matt Murphy), of whom Sam said, "He was so young, but the way he played, it sounded like two guitars." The rhythmic result was much the same, though Rufus's rough-voiced holler didn't have the same winsome appeal as Little Junior Parker, nor did the record enjoy the same commercial success. In fact, Rufus would not see any further commercial success for another ten years, when his "Walkin' the Dog" hit on the Stax label, actually going to number 10 on the pop charts and inspiring a cover version by the Rolling Stones. But "Tiger Man" was full of enough rough fun, energy, and sass to inspire a young Elvis Presley to try to cover it on Sun a couple of years later in a version that is lost to history, then incorporate it as a staple of his act when he returned to live performing in Las Vegas in 1969. For me, one of the most vivid memories connected to the song was witnessing Rufus's son, Marvell, a gifted musician much sought-after as a keyboard player but never as a singer, strut the stage and bellow out the song as uninhibitedly as his father at the grand opening of the Country Music Hall of Fame's exhibit and tribute to Sam Phillips and Sun Records in 2012.

SOFTLY AND TENDERLY/ MY GOD IS REAL
The Prisonaires
(Confined to the Tennessee State Prison, Nashville, Tenn.)

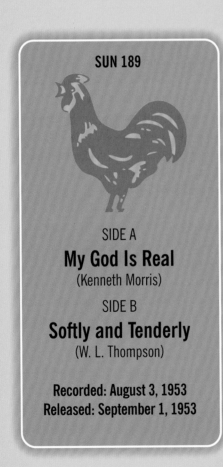

SUN 189

SIDE A
My God Is Real
(Kenneth Morris)

SIDE B
Softly and Tenderly
(W. L. Thompson)

Recorded: August 3, 1953
Released: September 1, 1953

Left: The Prisonaires on the air at WSOK—Nashville's first Black radio station.

Prisonaires' lead tenor Johnny Bragg always told the story about the woebegone young White boy who was hanging around the studio at the Prisonaires' epochal first recording session. In some versions of the story the boy was wielding a broom, in others he was just pestering Sam Phillips; in the most familiar version he helped Johnny with his phrasing during a break—all right, you guessed it: the boy was Elvis Presley. And none of it is true, although Elvis did indeed befriend Bragg a few years later, when he was back in prison after getting a governor's pardon and early release.

What does appear to be true is that Elvis read the newspaper story about the Prisonaires' first recording session and came in shortly after their second on August 3, 1953, at which they recorded two gospel numbers, this time with Ike Turner helping out on piano. Quite unexpectedly they gave "Softly and Tenderly," which is ordinarily taken at a sedate pace, an up-tempo handclapping treatment, with Ike's boogie piano leading the way. "My God Is Real," with just William Stewart's guitar and Johnny Bragg's pure, undistilled vocal lead, is more along the lines of what fans of the first record (*see p. 91*) might have expected, but in a surprising miscalculation Sam released the record at the very moment that "Just Walkin' in the Rain" broke into the R&B Top 10, and the coincidence of timing didn't do either the record, or the Prisonaires' career, any good.

And Elvis Presley's connection to all this? Well, in a story that might otherwise have been little more than a footnote, he showed up in August of 1953 and paid $4 to cut a two-sided acetate, ostensibly to hear the sound of his own voice, though his real reason was almost certainly to be "discovered" by Sam Phillips, the man the newspaper article described as open to every sort of talent. One side of the acetate that Elvis recorded at the Memphis Recording Service was "That's When Your Heartaches Begin," an Ink Spots number featuring the voice of Bill Kenny, Johnny Bragg's inspiration, and the boy's, too. Elvis was not discovered on this occasion; in fact, it would take another ten months before he came to Sam Phillips's attention at all. But when Marion Keisker packaged his acetate and presented him with his bill, she used the back of a label that had just been printed for the Prisonaires' next release, which would not come out until September 1, 1953, and you can barely discern "Softly and Tenderly" peeping out from underneath the white typed label.

Blues Vocal
2:20

emphis Music
U-89 BMI

MYSTERY TRAIN
(Parker)
LITTLE JUNIOR'S
BLUE FLAMES
192

MEMPHIS, TENNESSEE.

LOVE MY BABY/ MYSTERY TRAIN
Little Junior's Blue Flames

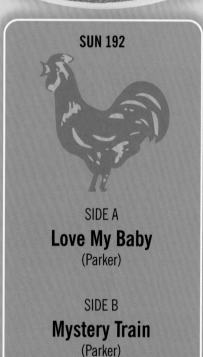

SUN 192

SIDE A
Love My Baby
(Parker)

SIDE B
Mystery Train
(Parker)

Recorded: August 5, 1953
Released: November 1, 1953

Right: Junior Parker (second from left) with Bobby Bland (left, squatting) and guitarist Pat Hare (right).

Far right: Studio portrait of Junior Parker.

Here we have the prototype for everything that was to follow. (I hope you're not tired of my saying this by now, but it's true—many times over.) Once again, listen to the rhythm—actually, listen to the rhythms of both sides, first the slightly delayed train rhythm of "Mystery Train," which subscribes to one of Sam Phillips's favorite anticipatory rhythmic patterns (check out Carl Perkins's "Blue Suede Shoes" for a point of reference), then the flyaway, let-it-all-out momentum of "Love My Baby," driven once again by Floyd Murphy's house-wrecking guitar, which Sam would subsequently use as a tutorial for virtually every young White guitarist who came into his studio. And if all that doesn't get you, see if you can resist the sly, insinuating vocal of Little Junior himself, a cousin by affinity if not by lineage of Al Green, who dedicated his ineffable "Take Me to the River" to "a cousin of mine, Little Junior Parker." In a sense this may be Sam Phillips's most "perfect" two-sided single (well, maybe not, how about Howlin' Wolf's first release?), little as I'm sure you are aware by now he would care for the appellation. But it is. Perfect.

IF LOVIN' IS BELIEVING
Billy "The Kid" Emerson

SUN 195

SIDE A
No Teasing Around
(Emerson)

SIDE B
If Lovin' Is Believing
(Emerson)

Recorded: January 11, 1954
Released: February 20, 1954

*Left: Billy and his wife, Camilla, on their
wedding day, June 6, 1955, in Biloxi, Mississippi.*

Another eccentric track by another eccentric talent. This was recorded at Billy "The Kid" Emerson's first session in January 1954 with Ike Turner, who had recently discovered him playing piano in Florida, leading his own St. Louis–based band on heavily distorted guitar. The record was initially released on Sam's brand-new "audition" label, Flip, then virtually simultaneously on Sun. There are certainly other, better Billy "The Kid" sides, but like all of Emerson's work it is strikingly original both in its lyrics and, even more, in its arrangement (it's hard to say whether the credit should go to Emerson or Ike Turner here). The rhythm seems slow to build, maybe even a little sludgy at times, but it is accompanied by Emerson's characteristically strong vocal and clever lyrics, and obviously it had something, or why else would it have been taken as an almost exact model for Bob Dylan's 2020 "False Prophet"? It would be well worth listening to a whole album of Billy "The Kid" Emerson's distinctive compositions (in later years he would cowrite "Dead Presidents" for Little Walter) but, given its pedigree, this would be a good place to start.

WOLF CALL BOOGIE
Hot Shot Love

SUN 196

SIDE A
Wolf Call Boogie
(Love)

SIDE B
Harmonica Jam
(Love)

Recorded: January 8, 1954
Released: February 20, 1954

While we're on the subject of eccentrics (and remember, this is a term of the highest praise in the vocabulary of Sam Phillips, who could with justice have prided himself on being the greatest eccentric of them all), let us not forget Hot Shot Love's "Wolf Call Boogie," recorded just three days before Billy "The Kid" Emerson's debut session and released on the same day. Coy "Hot Shot" Love was a sign painter (he advertised both his sign painting and his distinctive philosophy on the back of the bicycle he rode all around the streets of South Memphis), whose approach to harmonica, for all of its heavy amplification, would hardly have been out of place in a 1920s "race" recording catalogue.

In some ways this is a cousin to "the dozens," with Love conducting a dialogue with himself much in the manner of some of Bo Diddley's comic interchanges with his maracas player, Jerome Green, or even John Lee Hooker's running monologue with himself in "Boogie Chillen." But it is the whoops and hollers and hard harmonica-blowing that stand out, along with Pat Hare's guitar and a rackety rhythm section led by studio janitor and piano player Mose Vinson, who also played on Jimmy DeBerry's "Take a Little Chance" and James Cotton's "Cotton Crop Blues" (*see p. 111*). One thing to note: Sam Phillips did not believe in fades, and even this semi-chaotic venture comes to a conclusory end.

Right: Hot Shot Love.

TROUBLESOME WATERS
Howard Seratt

SUN 198

SIDE A
Troublesome Waters
(Rippetoe)

SIDE B
I Must Be Saved
(Coats)

Recorded: Late 1953
Released: February 20, 1954

"**Troublesome Waters,**" **while recorded in late 1953,** was the third Sun single released on February 20, 1954, and probably the least commercial, which if you look at the two previous selections, is really saying something. (Just remember, we're getting very close to July 5, 1954, the date of Elvis Presley's commercial recording debut.) Howard Seratt, in Sam's mind, possessed one of the most affecting voices he had ever heard. ("Oh, that man! I never heard a person, no matter what category of music, could sing as beautifully.") Born and raised on a farm outside Manila, Arkansas, he contracted polio before the age of two and remained on crutches for the rest of his life. He taught himself harmonica and guitar at an early age, sang in a hillbilly band during World War II, and then, after a religious conversion, turned to spiritual music exclusively. To his great regret, Sam could see no commercial potential in his music and tried half-heartedly to persuade Seratt to record secular songs—but he was not-even-close-to-secretly gratified that he did not. So strong, in fact, was his belief in Seratt, in both the strength of his conviction and the purity of his voice, that, in the spring of 1953, Sam brought him to Nashville to sing for Governor Clement and help persuade the governor to allow Sam to record the Prisonaires. The governor was completely won over, as I think you will be by this one-of-a-kind recording, as surprising in its own way as "Just Walkin' in the Rain" (*see p. 83*)—further proof, if proof were needed, of the multiplicity and multidimensionality of the talent on the Sun label.

Right: Howard Seratt shaking hands with Tennessee Governor Frank Clement. The Rev. C. O. Ray (left) and Sam Phillips look on.

Rev. C. O. Ray
Bismarck, North Dakota

Honorable
Frank G. Clement
Governor Of Tennessee

Howard Seratt

Sam C. Phillips, President
Sun Records, Inc.

LOOK TO JESUS / EVERY NIGHT
The Jones Brothers

SUN 213

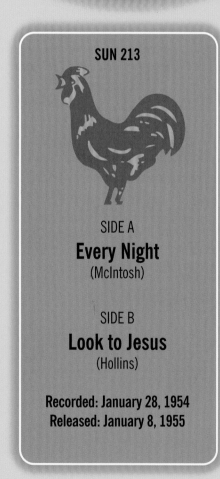

SIDE A
Every Night
(McIntosh)

SIDE B
Look to Jesus
(Hollins)

Recorded: January 28, 1954
Released: January 8, 1955

Whatever its dimensionality, it should be abundantly clear by now that Sam was not at all sure at this juncture which way to turn to consolidate the commercial ground he had gained. Gospel had been one of his first loves, and at around the same time that he recorded Howard Seratt, he was also recording the Jones Brothers, a hard-driving Black gospel quartet who possessed the kind of untrammeled spiritual fervor that always excited him. "Every Night," with its building intensity, is clearly in the more modern quartet style of the Soul Stirrers and the Dixie Hummingbirds, but it springs from the same sounds that Sam first heard as a boy spilling out of the small Black church just half a block from his own church in North Florence, Alabama. It seemed sometimes, Sam said, that when he stood outside the open windows of Armstead Methodist Chapel, it was as if the life force had entered his soul. It was the purity of human endeavor, the raw beauty of the human voice, that the preacher's words proclaimed, and the congregation's testimony echoed—it was the individuated nature of spiritual and musical and creative expression that he had first glimpsed working in the fields on his father's farm, before they were forced by the Depression to move to town. If he could have captured that alone, he said, he would have been happy to the end of his days, but he could never figure out a way to sell it. The Jones Brothers release did not come out until January 8, 1955 (Elvis Presley's twentieth birthday and just after the release of his third Sun single), almost a year after it was recorded. It was the only gospel quartet recording ever released on the Sun label.

Right: The Jones Brothers.

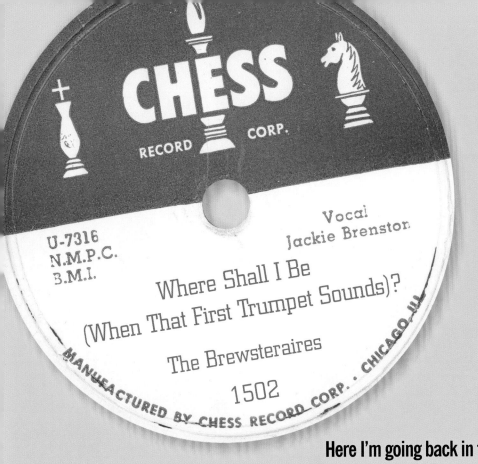

WHERE SHALL I BE (When That First Trumpet Sounds)?
The Brewsteraires

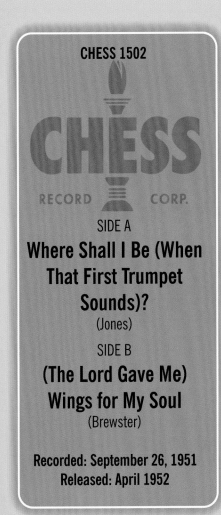

CHESS 1502

SIDE A
Where Shall I Be (When That First Trumpet Sounds)?
(Jones)

SIDE B
(The Lord Gave Me) Wings for My Soul
(Brewster)

Recorded: September 26, 1951
Released: April 1952

Left: The Brewsteraires. Clockwise from front: Melvin Lee (with guitar), D. K. Rogers, Nathaniel Peck, John Cole (lead), Sol Ousten, and Henry Reed.

Here I'm going back in time, just to make—well, to reiterate, really—a point. This was recorded in 1951 by the Brewsteraires, one of the principal vehicles that Dr. W. H. Brewster, pastor of East Trigg Baptist Church, used to put across his musical message. Dr. Brewster was not only a renowned gospel composer (he wrote Mahalia Jackson's magisterial "Move On Up a Little Higher" and Clara Ward's "Surely God Is Able," among many other gospel standards as enduring in their own way as Sam Cooke's "A Change Is Gonna Come") but also a prominent civil rights leader whose frequently performed plays and pageants always featured an uplifting political and social theme. "I was trying to inspire Black people to move up higher," Dr. Brewster said disarmingly of his music. He wrote the songs and pageants, he said, "for the common people who could not understand political language, who didn't know anything about economics."

It probably shouldn't be necessary to point out that Sam was a great admirer of Dr. Brewster, for his oratory as much as for his music, and he never missed the Sunday night broadcast of his church service on WHBQ if he could help it. Elvis Presley was just as much an admirer, and as a teenager he and his girlfriend, Dixie Locke, snuck out of their own service at the Assembly of God church around the corner to hear Dr. Brewster, who in later years would always speak glowingly of the music and character of the young man he first met in this manner and with whom he maintained a life-long acquaintance.

"Where Shall I Be (When That First Trumpet Sounds)?" in particular is a beautifully paced, beautifully articulated and modulated a cappella performance with echoes of the Golden Gate Quartet, and in theory it might have led to more recordings from Brewster's flock, including solo recordings by East Trigg's renowned soloist, Queen C. Anderson, an early model for Aretha Franklin, as was Brewster himself for her father, Reverend C. L. Franklin, during his years in Memphis.

Along with the Brewsteraires, Sam recorded other gospel groups such as the Memphis Travelers, the Evangelist Gospel Singers of Alabama, and the Gospel Tones early on, but he never subsequently returned to this, because, once again, he simply couldn't see a way to sell it. And so the recordings of Howard Seratt, the Prisonaires, the Jones Brothers, and one or two others stand virtually alone on Sun as pure professions of religious belief, as opposed to the spiritual faith with which, from Sam's point of view, *all* of his best recordings were imbued.

MY KIND OF CARRYING ON
Doug Poindexter

SUN 202

SIDE A
Now She Cares No More
(Moore–Deckelman–Moore)

SIDE B
My Kind of Carrying On
(Moore–Poindexter)

Recorded: ca. April 13, 1954
Released: May 1, 1954

Left: Doug Poindexter (center) with the Starlite Wranglers. From left: Bill Black, Tommy Sealey, Poindexter, Millard Yow on steel guitar, Clyde Rush, and Scotty Moore.

It was with the hillbilly band, the Starlite Wranglers, that guitarist Scotty Moore, not too long out of the Navy and a hatter at his brother's dry-cleaning establishment, first entered the Sun studio in April 1954. It was Scotty's group, to which he had only recently recruited vocalist Doug Poindexter, a baker with a passion for Hank Williams. Poindexter, in fact, was the first to learn of Sam Phillips and his studio, and when they came in to audition Sam thought he heard something a little bit different. Most of all, though, he connected with their twenty-two-year-old leader, who started stopping by the studio nearly every day after work to talk about (or maybe mostly to listen to) Sam's ideas about the future. "Sam knew there was a crossover coming," Scotty said. "He foresaw it. I think that recording all those Black artists had to give him an insight. He just didn't know where that insight would lead."

"My Kind of Carrying On," the new band's signature number, was a cheerfully up-tempo, and slightly off-color, tune that Scotty had written. What distinguished it most to Sam's ears was the interaction between Moore and bass player Bill Black, as well as the bright rhythmic sound of the guitar as it opened with a jaunty take-off on Nashville guitar virtuoso Chet Atkins's thumb-picking style.

The other element that would come to distinguish the record upon its release was its *sound*. This was one of the very first times that Sam tried out an idea he had just come up with, a kind of artificial echo that he achieved by running the initial taped recording simultaneously through a second recorder and thereby creating a controlled delay. Artificial echo was in the air by the early '50s (Les Paul would be the most prominent example), but without a giant studio in which to create it Sam felt his homemade device created an even greater richness of effect, a more "natural" approximation of the way the music actually sounded when you heard it in a crowded honky-tonk or bar. He called his invention "slapback," and it would almost immediately become the hallmark of the Sun sound.

The record didn't sell, and Scotty soon decided Doug Poindexter was not the right person to front the band, but he continued his conversations with Sam Phillips, and a few weeks later Sam started talking to him about a young kid that he thought might have something different. On July 3, 1954, he had Scotty get in touch with the boy for an audition at his house. When the young man showed up, Scotty's wife, Bobbie, opened the door and was taken aback to discover a pimply-faced boy "wearing a black shirt, pink pants with a black stripe, white shoes, and a greasy ducktail." They ran through every song that he knew, it seemed, and Scotty called Sam and told him he thought the kid showed promise. The next day Elvis Presley was back in the studio with Scotty and his bandmate and neighbor, Bill Black, for his first recording session.

I'VE BEEN DECEIVED/ PEEPIN' EYES
Charlie Feathers

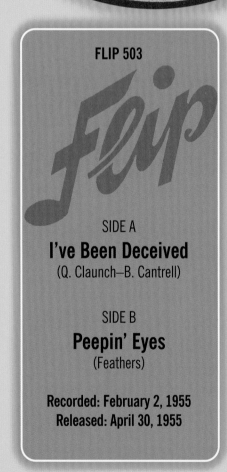

FLIP 503

SIDE A
I've Been Deceived
(Q. Claunch–B. Cantrell)

SIDE B
Peepin' Eyes
(Feathers)

Recorded: February 2, 1955
Released: April 30, 1955

Right: Charlie Feathers.

Inset: Charlie Feathers with Jerry Huffman and Shorty Torrance (standing); Quinton Claunch and Jody Chastain (seated).

Here is yet another direction Sun Records might have taken during that indeterminate time in 1954 and early 1955 before fate could be said to have fully stepped in. Charlie Feathers was as anguished a hillbilly singer as anyone in the post–Hank Williams era, as extravagantly gifted as anyone on the Sun roster—and as determinedly eccentric. He grew up schooled on the bluegrass of Bill Monroe and the blues of local musician Junior Kimbrough but, for all his talent, he never seemed able to carve out an identity for himself. In later years he would claim to have "invented rockabilly"—in his version of the story it was Elvis who took his inspiration from Charlie rather than the other way around.

Here, in the earliest days of his career, after Elvis had already established his style on Sun, Sam assigned Feathers to Quinton Claunch and Bill Cantrell, two country musicians whom he knew from his radio days in Florence. In the early days of 1955, Sam seems to have thought that there was still room for an independent country line on Sun, and he put out records by a number of promising young hillbilly artists, including Carl Perkins, under Claunch and Cantrell's direction. They rehearsed the singers, then delivered them to Sam fully prepared, with all the songs selected and ready to be played by a band that included Cantrell on "corn-stalk" fiddle, Claunch playing "tic-tac" rhythm on his electric guitar, and, generally, Stan Kesler on steel guitar.

With this single, Charlie Feathers certainly delivered two hard-edged performances (think George Jones without any filter between inspiration and execution), but what they got in the studio, complete with yelps, hiccoughs, and the propensity to stretch out his syllables like a damn gospel singer, was only a tenth of what Sam was convinced he had to offer. On the other hand, he wasn't sure that Charlie had the temperament to fully realize his potential. According to Quinton Claunch, a great champion of Charlie's talent, "He was his own worst enemy. He didn't trust anybody. [It was like] he'd wake up in a new world every morning." Or as Bill Cantrell put it: "If that guy just had a little education and a little common sense, he could've been where Carl Perkins got." But despite some remarkable rockabilly sides on the King label over the next year or two, Feathers not surprisingly never did get to that place, though he definitely created a legend of his own.

GONNA DANCE ALL NIGHT
Hardrock Gunter

SUN 201

SIDE A
Fallen Angel
(H. Gunter)

SIDE B
Gonna Dance All Night
(H. Gunter)

Recorded: Unknown
Released: May 1, 1954

Left: Hardrock Gunter.

Sam first heard of Hardrock Gunter through his brother-in-law Jimmy Connolly who had hired Sam as a radio announcer at Florence radio station WLAY in 1942, his first full-time job. (They were not quite brothers-in-law yet.) Connolly was a radio pioneer in his own right, who in 1949 started a show on the Birmingham radio station that he was then managing called *The Atomic Boogie Hour*, whose primary focus, very much like Dewey Phillips's *Red Hot and Blu*e, was rhythm and blues.

Sidney "Hardrock" Gunter worked at the station in various capacities while pursuing a musical career that began in country music but by 1950 had moved over to boogie-woogie-proto-rock 'n' roll with a hillbilly flavor. ("We're Gonna Rock 'n' Roll, We're Gonna Dance All Night" was the original title of one of his earliest recordings, though by the time it was released, all but the last four words had been dropped.) By 1954 Hardrock was thinking of re-recording that song, and Jimmy Connolly, who shared Sam's vision of a new musical day, thought it would be perfect for the Sun label. Sam was sold on the song and tried to get Gunter to come to Memphis to record, but Hardrock, as his name might suggest, possessed a stubborn streak and cut it in Birmingham, sending Sam the master in February 1954. It wasn't really what Sam wanted, he was sure he could have done better, but it rocked some, even with its still-truncated title, and Sam released it on May 1, 1954, the same day the Starlite Wranglers record (*see p. 105*) came out.

COTTON CROP BLUES
James Cotton

"Cotton Crop Blues" was released on July 1, 1954, along with Harmonica Frank's "Rockin' Chair Daddy" (*see p. 112*)—which goes to show that Sam Phillips may have been inching toward a new synthesis but he still wasn't sure he had hit on the right formula yet. Cotton, just nineteen years old, had made his recording debut on a Howlin' Wolf session two years earlier and would go on to become the second-most-celebrated harmonica player in Muddy Waters's seminal Chicago blues band (Little Walter, of course, was the first), but Sam recorded him here in a configuration that eliminated the harmonica and focused on Cotton's vocal and the manic, overamplified guitar of sometime Blue Flame Pat Hare. Though the song was based on a Roosevelt Sykes recording from the early 1930s, and despite the fact that Pat Hare's playing served as yet another marker on the road to rockabilly, with the singer's unadorned vocal delivery "Cotton Crop Blues" could very well be taken as a song of implicit social protest against a system that had for so long exerted a vice grip on the lives of Southern Blacks.

Left: James Cotton, c. 1960s.

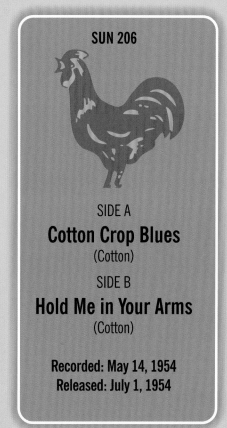

SUN 206

SIDE A
Cotton Crop Blues
(Cotton)

SIDE B
Hold Me in Your Arms
(Cotton)

Recorded: May 14, 1954
Released: July 1, 1954

ROCKIN' CHAIR DADDY
Harmonica Frank

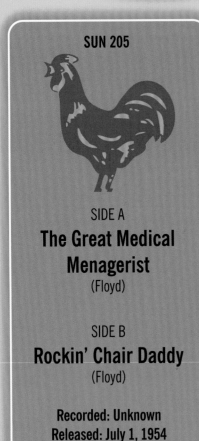

SUN 205

SIDE A
The Great Medical Menagerist
(Floyd)

SIDE B
Rockin' Chair Daddy
(Floyd)

Recorded: Unknown
Released: July 1, 1954

I may have overemphasized the word "eccentricity" (and you can substitute "individuality" if you like—or Sam's favorite formulation, "individualism *in the extreme*"), but you can't avoid the term when talking about Harmonica Frank, a grizzled White medicine show veteran in his forties who accompanied himself on harmonica and guitar. And, notably, played the harmonica without making use of either his hands or a harmonica rack, simply by rolling the instrument around in his mouth as he declaimed the lyrics of his blues and humorous entertainments in a parched, self-amused voice. He was, Sam said, "a beautiful hobo. He was short, fat, very abstract—and you looked at him and you really didn't know what he was thinking, what he was going to say or sing next. He had the greatest mind of his own—I think hobos by nature have to have that—and that fascinated me from the beginning. And then he had some of these old rhymes and tales and stuff that he had embellished, and some of them were so old, God, I guess they were old when my father was a kid." The subject at hand here, "Rockin' Chair Daddy" (and, no, the rocking part was not accidental) might best be described as a blues novelty tune, complete with growls, yowls, and odd twists of phrase, while the other side, "The Great Medical Menagerist," is a Woody Guthrie–type talking blues recounting medicine show days and including patter that gives every evidence of some of the hoary origins that Sam references above.

Right: Harmonica Frank.

Left: The box holding the master recording of "Rockin' Chair Daddy."

THAT'S ALL RIGHT
Elvis Presley

SUN 209

SIDE A
That's All Right
(Arthur Crudup)
SIDE B
Blue Moon of Kentucky
(Bill Monroe)

Recorded: July 5 and July 7, 1954
Released: July 19, 1954

Left: One of the most famous images in rock 'n' roll history, taken onstage in Tampa, July 31, 1955. It would become the cover of Elvis's first album for RCA.

This really *is* it: the revolution that Sam had both been predicting and searching for had finally arrived. It may or may not represent the moment that rock 'n' roll was born (it doesn't)—but it is without question the birth of something new.

Everyone knows the story, but it is no less startling in the retelling. Scotty Moore gave Elvis his audition on July 4, 1954—Elvis sang mostly ballads and country songs, just about every song he knew, and Scotty was impressed enough to recommend that they schedule a studio session the next night so Sam could hear for himself. The session did not go well. Elvis sang his heart out, desperate to take advantage of the opportunity he had been given, but somehow nothing clicked, and everyone was on the verge of going home (they all had jobs to go to the next day) when all of a sudden Elvis picked up his guitar and started beating on it and singing an old blues that Sam knew but none of them even suspected was in his repertoire. Scotty and bassist Bill Black soon fell in, and Sam, who had been dithering at the board (a technique he had employed at least since Howlin' Wolf first entered his studio—he didn't want the musicians to pay any attention to him, he wanted them above all to be *themselves*) suddenly snapped to. "What are you doing?" Sam said. "We don't know," said Scotty. "Well, back up," said Sam, "try to find a place to start, and do it again."

The song was "That's All Right," an up-tempo number originally recorded by Arthur "Big Boy" Crudup in 1946, and it came together so perfectly, so seemingly accidentally (though Sam didn't believe in either perfection or accidents), so pure in its essence, that there was almost nothing to do with it but get it down on tape. Sam didn't touch it, didn't add slapback, didn't call for more than one or two takes. And it's just as timeless today as it was then, and just as uncategorizable. Is it folk music? Is it rock 'n' roll? Is it country-flavored blues? It is, simply, itself.

It caught on instantly, became a turntable hit (DJ Dewey Phillips's turntable)—caught on so fast in fact that by the next day Sam was desperate for a B-side so he could put out the record. After a number of attempts over the next couple of days, Bill Black finally came up with the idea of doing much the same thing with a country number that they had done on the Arthur Crudup blues. He started "beating on his bass and singing 'Blue Moon of Kentucky' in a high falsetto voice," Scotty said, "more or less mimicking Bill Monroe [this was Bill Monroe's classic bluegrass tune, which was, in Monroe's version, a waltz], and Elvis started banging on the guitar, playing rhythm and singing, and I joined in and it just gelled." Sam applied a *lot* of slapback this time, he slathered it on in a way that he rarely would again, so the sound bounces around, and the lyrics chase each other in a manner far removed from Sam's conception of "more natural" natural sound. But of course, it was in its own way a classic, too, and one that would go on to influence so much of what was still to come.

THE BOOGIE DISEASE
Doctor Ross

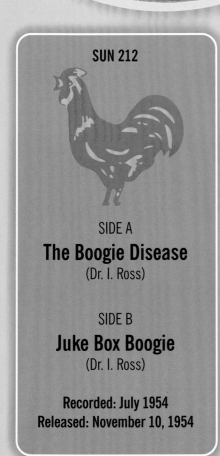

SIDE A
The Boogie Disease
(Dr. I. Ross)

SIDE B
Juke Box Boogie
(Dr. I. Ross)

Recorded: July 1954
Released: November 10, 1954

And here we're presented with one more strand in the origins of rock 'n' roll in the infectious "Boogie Disease" of "Doctor" Isaiah Ross (pun certainly intended), released in the fall of 1954, not long after Elvis's second Sun single. Doctor Ross, a twenty-nine-year old native of Tunica, Mississippi, had first recorded for Sam three years earlier, and was yet another unregenerate disciple of John Lee Hooker. He was always boogieing, but this was perhaps his purest representation of the form. As Jimmy DeBerry had earlier proclaimed, "Even little babies boppin'/Poppin' their little fingers, too," and there was no one more rocking than Doctor Ross, like Harmonica Frank, though in a very different vein, a one-man guitar-and-harmonica, plus drums, band (though not here). His prescription was simple in this case. "Boogie for the doctor / Boogie for the nurse / I'm gonna keep on boogiein' / Till they throw me in the hearse." And once again we see the faith invested in the John Lee Hooker prototype by both him and Sam. As "Boogie Chillen" was the first to proclaim, "Let that boy boogie woogie, it's in him, and it's gotta come out."

Left: Dr. Ross with his family,
Flint, Michigan, 1955.

Vocal
U-139

Hi-Lo Music
BMI

WHEN IT RAINS IT POURS
(Emerson)
BILLY (The Kid) EMERSON

214

MEMPHIS, TENNESSEE

SUN 214

SIDE A
Move Baby Move
(Emerson)

SIDE B
When It Rains It Pours
(Emerson)

Recorded: October 27, 1954
Released: January 8, 1955

WHEN IT RAINS IT POURS
Billy "The Kid" Emerson

Once again it is not so much the singer as the song, and once again the singer/composer is Billy "The Kid" Emerson. This is probably a better song than his initial offering—a *great* song—and one that calls out to be covered. In this case the call was answered most prominently by Elvis Presley, who tried a number of times (including during his Sun sojourn), although he never could quite get it to his own satisfaction. Like many blues it is a song of genuine simplicity, with a great hook, that offers many different avenues of approach.

Right: Billy "The Kid" Emerson studio portrait.

Vocal
U-140

Leeds
Ascap

MILKCOW BLUES BOOGIE
(Arnold)
ELVIS PRESLEY
SCOTTY and BILL
215
MEMPHIS, TENNESSEE

MILKCOW BLUES BOOGIE/ YOU'RE A HEART BREAKER
Elvis Presley

This was Elvis's third single, released just one week before "When It Rains It Pours." By now Elvis was a Memphis byword (the previous summer Memphis teenagers were said to have adopted the scatted chorus of his first single as a form of greeting), and a star of the Louisiana Hayride, Shreveport's answer to the Grand Ole Opry. This is a wonderful example of Elvis's unfettered exuberance on the one hand, and of his calculated craft, too. Originally a blues from the '30s by Kokomo Arnold ("Milk Cow Blues"), it had been covered many times over the years, most notably in western swing versions by Bob Wills and his brother Johnnie Lee. Here Elvis makes it his own, with a beautiful slow beginning that should prove once and for all what a great blues singer he could be. But then he announces, "Hold it, fellas, that don't move me, let's get real, real gone for a change." And they do.

An interesting side note: the other side, "You're a Heartbreaker," was Elvis's first pop original, a bright countryish number that Sam picked up from a theater manager in Covington, Tennessee, and to which he imparted a lilting swing.

Left: Selling Elvis: an early ad.

Far left: Elvis, Scotty, and Bill at Messick High School in Memphis, January 1955.

ELVIS PRESLEY
HIS ORIGINAL RECORD OF
"THAT'S ALL RIGHT" WAS
MEMPHIS' BIGGEST C & W
RECORD IN 1954.
COMPARE!
YOU'LL PICK IT!
NEW RELEASE
"You're A Heartbreaker"
"Milk Cow Blues Boogie"
DJ'S—DISTRIBUTORS
CALL SUN RECORDS
MEMPHIS, TENN.
For Tours—Shows
Personal Appearances
Write — Wire — Call
Exclusive Personal Management
BOB NEAL
160 UNION AVE.,
MEMPHIS, TENN.

SUN 215

SIDE A
Milkcow Blues Boogie
(Arnold)

SIDE B
You're a Heartbreaker
(Jack Sallee)

Recorded: November/ December 1954
Released: December 29, 1954

Johnny Cash and the Tennessee Two.

"I am a sound freak.
I could play around
with sound forever."

—Sam Phillips

BABY LET'S PLAY HOUSE/ I'M LEFT, YOUR'E RIGHT, SHE'S GONE
Elvis Presley

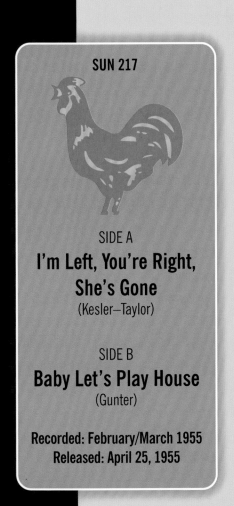

SUN 217

SIDE A
I'm Left, You're Right, She's Gone
(Kesler–Taylor)

SIDE B
Baby Let's Play House
(Gunter)

Recorded: February/March 1955
Released: April 25, 1955

Under any other circumstances this might be considered the apogee of Elvis's Sun career—but there's another one coming, just three places down. As revolutionary as any of Elvis's Sun singles, "Baby Let's Play House" introduces a note of pure play not readily apparent in the first three. From its opening notes, it sets a tone of bubbling irrepressibility not even hinted at in the R&B original. "Oh, baby, baby, baby, baby, baby," Elvis declares with a brand-new hiccoughing stutter that just knocked Sam out (not to mention Buddy Holly, who saw Elvis perform numerous times in Lubbock, Texas, in his own pre-stardom days) with its utterly uninhibited, unpredictable, insensate declaration of joy.

Once again, the other side, "I'm Left, You're Right, She's Gone," this one cowritten by ubiquitous Memphis steel guitar player Stan Kesler, strikes a cheerful pop tone in the face of heartbreak, indicating one of the ways it would seem Sam Phillips was thinking of expanding his artist's commercial horizons.

Left: Elvis beckoning the crowd, c. 1955.

I FEEL SO WORRIED
Sammy Lewis-Willie Johnson Combo

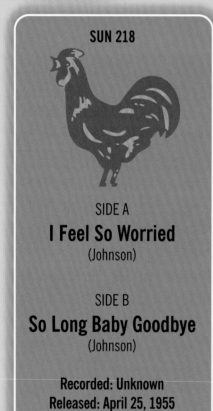

SUN 218

SIDE A
I Feel So Worried
(Johnson)

SIDE B
So Long Baby Goodbye
(Johnson)

Recorded: Unknown
Released: April 25, 1955

You remember "Boogie Chillen"? Well, here it comes again in yet another devastating guise under the name of "I Feel So Worried." And here's Willie Johnson again, Howlin' Wolf's original guitarist, the first in what by now had become a distinguished line of over-the-top, smolderingly overamplified players. The first time he heard Willie Johnson, Sam said, he was astonished not just by the attack but by the subtlety of his playing, which combined lead and rhythm in a combination of thick, clotted chords and deftly distorted single-string runs.

But it wasn't just that—he wasn't beyond throwing in bebop inflections, along with echoes of T-Bone Walker's delicate phrasing, and, most important of all, delivering the dirtiest sound you could ever imagine being drawn from an electric guitar. Here he is joined by harmonica player and vocalist Sammy Lewis, and together they create a sound so explosive that when Willie calls out, "Blow the backs off it, Sammy," you feel like he really *will*.

Left: The box holding the master recording of "I Feel So Worried."

Right: Sammy Lewis, c.1970.

HEY, PORTER!
Johnny Cash and the Tennessee Two

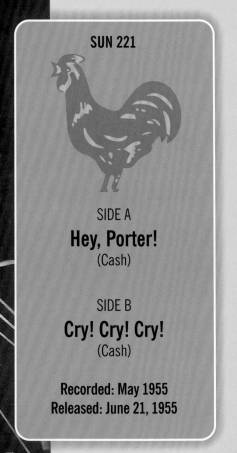

SUN 221

SIDE A
Hey, Porter!
(Cash)

SIDE B
Cry! Cry! Cry!
(Cash)

Recorded: May 1955
Released: June 21, 1955

Left: Johnny Cash—his first publicity shot.

Johnny Cash arrived at the Sun studio at the invitation of Elvis Presley in early 1955. He had seen Elvis perform the previous fall at the grand opening of Katz Drugstore. Recently arrived in Memphis after a three-year hitch in the Air Force, Cash was studying to be a radio announcer, but he had recently put a small group together. He did not receive a warm welcome. Marion Keisker told him Sam didn't have time for him, he was too busy with Elvis, and then when he finally did get the opportunity to present himself to Mr. Phillips and told him he was a gospel singer, Sam explained to him the same thing he had already told others: he just didn't have any way to sell it.

Finally, after an arduous series of try-outs in which John, or J. R., Cash ("Johnny" was adopted for his first release because Sam said it sounded better than "John" if you were looking to appeal to young people) ran through just about every type of song he knew, including a few originals. Sam was particularly taken with one he had written as a poem while he was still stationed in Germany. There may have been a note of homesickness still detectable in its lyrics. But what saved it from anything remotely approaching sentimentality was the excitement and exuberance of its tone. In addition to which, Cash's distinctive baritone, and the churning train rhythm, the "boom-chick-a boom" sound that John and his two accompanying musicians, both neophytes on their instruments (guitar and string bass), imparted to it. All of which made for a glorious ride home, only further enlivened by the sharply tuned interchange of humor, wordplay, and observation in Cash's lyrics.

It was, the way Sam heard it, like a traditional folk song as sung by Burl Ives, but with more bite to it and a hard-won musical arrangement that had been agonizingly put together note by note. There was something reassuringly familiar about it, and yet it was at the same time strikingly original, too. And then there was Cash himself: his commanding presence, his believability, the tremulous but unwavering sincerity of his voice. For Sam it was almost like discovering Howlin' Wolf: you might not *like* his voice, but you could not deny it.

The other side, "Cry! Cry! Cry!," turned out to be the *Billboard* hit, but both sides were regional successes and put Johnny Cash's name on the national map, where it would remain until the day of his death. Though, as Cash recalled, he felt little certainty about the future at the time. Sam gave him one of the first promotional copies of the record to bring to Elvis's manager, Memphis DJ Bob Neal, and Cash carried it like a baby bird. When Neal dropped it and it broke, he said, "I thought my world had ended. I didn't think they'd make another one!"

RED HOT
Billy "The Kid" Emerson

SUN 219

SIDE A
Red Hot
(Emerson)

SIDE B
No Greater Love
(Emerson)

Recorded: May 31, 1955
Released: June 21, 1955

Here once again we have Billy "The Kid" Emerson with another classic song, this time delivered over a rhumba-ish beat (not too far removed from the original "Hound Dog"—it was a fashionable style). The song's premise is pretty simple, just a straightahead (maybe a little boastful) declaration of pride in the singer's girlfriend, who is in every imaginable way "red hot." The record was "taking off big and going white [even though] other Emerson releases have been strictly for the Negro trade," Sam wrote to one of his distributors in the summer of 1955, with his abiding faith that the crossover was still as likely to take place going in this direction as the other.

Well, Sam was certainly right. Crossover was happening all over the place, particularly with the explosive pop success of Chuck Berry, Bo Diddley, Little Richard, and Ray Charles on other labels—but with "Red Hot" he would have to be satisfied with its enduring popularity in one cover version after another over the years (including Billy Riley's on Sun just two years later—*see p. 117*) and its permanent status as a rockabilly classic right up to the present day.

Left: Billy Emerson.

MYSTERY TRAIN/ I FORGOT TO REMEMBER TO FORGET
Elvis Presley

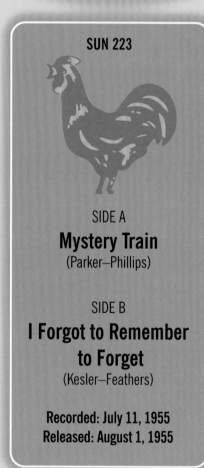

SUN 223

SIDE A
Mystery Train
(Parker–Phillips)

SIDE B
I Forgot to Remember to Forget
(Kesler–Feathers)

Recorded: July 11, 1955
Released: August 1, 1955

Right: Elvis in concert, c.1955.

Inset: Before he was the King of Rock 'n' Roll, Elvis was the "Most Promising Country & Western Artist."

Okay, can we call this the apogee? In many ways it might almost be seen as a replay of the moment in which "That's All Right" came together, so perfect in its imperfection— right down to Elvis's trailing-off laughter at the end—that like "That's All Right," it could not be retouched. There is no question that Little Junior Parker was one of Elvis's favorite artists, and "Mystery Train" may well have been Elvis's favorite Little Junior Parker song (*see p. 92*). And yet, however undeniable the inspiration, there is no question that he makes the song his own, just as he did every one of the songs he recorded for Sun.

Ironically, the genesis of Elvis's version was not in fact the Parker original, but "Love My Baby," the other side of Little Junior's record. That was the song that Sam presented to Elvis and guitarist Scotty Moore for their rhythmic model. From Sam's point of view he wasn't looking for Scotty to replicate what Floyd Murphy did on the original, what he was trying to do was to simply encourage Scotty to open up and play a little more on the "uncautious" side, to play with what he called "a not too perfectly scheduled anticipation." Which is exactly what he got on the only take of the song that survives and, for all we know, the only take that was attempted. As Sam said in one way or another on numerous occasions, how can you improve on perfect imperfection?

The other side, "I Forgot to Remember to Forget," was another catchy Stan Kesler original, nowhere near as sublime as "Mystery Train," but it was Elvis's first Top 10 national country hit, and perhaps the final inducement for RCA to put up an unprecedented $40,000 to purchase Elvis's contract from Sun.

One final note. Not long after the "Mystery Train" session in July, Elvis came in to record an obscure R&B song called "Tryin' to Get to You," while Sam was in the midst of negotiating the RCA sale. The song was never completed, because there was never another Sun session, and it was included in its very compelling, but still inchoate, state on Elvis's first, classic RCA album. The reason that I mention this is that sometimes when people ask which is my favorite Sun cut by Elvis, I say "Tryin' to Get to You," the next take, the one that never got recorded but would have captured the full breadth of the song's spiritual essence if it had, picking up on the spirit suggested by the last take they were able to do.

LET THE JUKEBOX KEEP ON PLAYING/ GONE, GONE, GONE
Carl Perkins

Carl Perkins was another of those raw-boned White country boys with a different mind-set who had started showing up at Sam's door, untried, unproven, and just as hungry for acceptance as many of the African-American artists he had recorded over the years. They were drawn, clearly, by the magnetism of Elvis Presley's talent—the music that came alive for them as soon as they heard it, suggesting not only common threads of aspiration and imagination but what it might mean both for their careers and their very sense of themselves.

Carl Perkins had been working as a baker in Jackson, Tennessee, playing music on the weekends, when his wife heard "That's All Right" on the radio. "That sounds a lot like you, Carl," she said. And that was what brought him to Sun. He had already been turned away by Marion Keisker and was just starting out the door when Sam arrived in a light-blue Cadillac and, with a sense of desperation, Perkins flung himself at the man who had discovered Elvis Presley.

As he would always vividly recall: "He said, 'I ain't got time.' I said, 'Mr. Phillips, please. Just one song. Will you?' I guess I said it just that hurt. He said, 'Okay, get set up. But I can't listen long.' We was set up and picking before he could get back to the control room. Afterwards he told me, 'I couldn't say no. Never have I [seen] a pitifuller-looking fellow as you looked when I said, "I'm too busy to listen to you." You overpowered me.' I said, 'I didn't mean to, but I'm glad I did.' That was the beginning right there."

His music was as deeply felt as he looked, as close to the next Hank Williams "if the world needed another Hank Williams," Sam said, as he had ever heard, and he assigned Carl to his new "country scouts," Quinton Claunch and Bill Cantrell (this was before they worked with Charlie Feathers). He put out the first release, which was pure, and pleading, hillbilly, on his "audition," Flip label, and the second, released in the summer of 1955, stayed in that heartbroken mode with "Let the Juke Box Keep on Playing." But it was "Gone, Gone, Gone," a traditional country-inflected blues with a kind of jump to it, that gave it a uniqueness that Sam had never heard from any other hillbilly singer ("That [guitar] was going to move somewhere that it didn't normally move") and that, for him, unmistakably suggested the future. Bill Cantrell's fiddle, barely audible because of the way Sam miked the session, echoes the sound of a blues harmonica, as Carl's buoyant vocal leaps right out of the mix. Little did anyone know that the future was to arrive just a few months later with the sale of Elvis's contract at the end of November. "You're my rocker now," Sam said to Carl, and the result was the next selection.

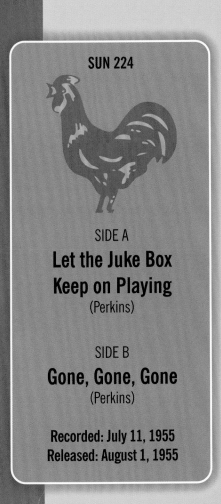

SUN 224

SIDE A
Let the Juke Box Keep on Playing
(Perkins)

SIDE B
Gone, Gone, Gone
(Perkins)

Recorded: July 11, 1955
Released: August 1, 1955

Left: Carl Perkins in an early studio portrait.

BLUE SUEDE SHOES
Carl Perkins

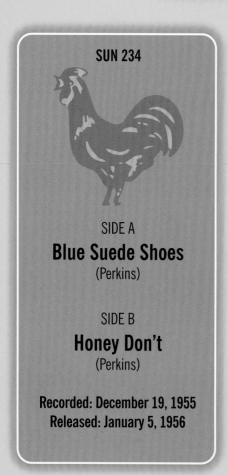

SUN 234

SIDE A
Blue Suede Shoes
(Perkins)

SIDE B
Honey Don't
(Perkins)

Recorded: December 19, 1955
Released: January 5, 1956

It was recorded less than a month after Elvis was formally signed by RCA, and along with Chuck Berry's "Johnny B. Goode" and just a few others, became one of the permanent anthems of the new, and newly named, rock 'n' roll movement. "Blue Suede Shoes" was first inspired by a conversation Carl Perkins had with his labelmate Johnny Cash, in which Cash described an air force buddy, C. V. White, who was meticulous about his appearance. One day they were all standing in the chowline when somebody stepped on C. V.'s toes. "Hey, man," said C. V. drily, who like everyone else was wearing regulation black air force–issue shoes, "I don't care what you do with my fräulein, [just] don't step on my blue suede shoes." Carl took it from there.

When it was released, the record exploded, rising faster than "Heartbreak Hotel," Elvis's first RCA release, and becoming the first song to reach the top of the pop, country, and R&B charts. Sam loved the song from the moment Carl first played it for him on the telephone, but it was the little rhythmic delay that Carl imparted to its delivery that for Sam gave the song its unique appeal. "You say a vamp is a vamp is a vamp. That's not true. Sure, you can change the tempo and all [that] stuff, but there's a certain feel on a vamp—once you get that thing going, it's kind of like the Hallelujah Chorus in a Black church." That was what he always felt was missing from Elvis's cover version on RCA—there was no slowdown, and no "Hallelujah Chorus."

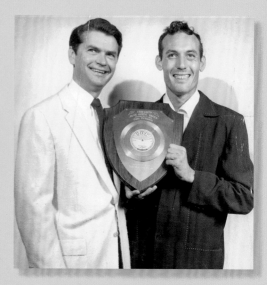

Far right: Carl holding the shoe that made him famous . . .

. . . and (right) the gold record he got for it.

THERE'S NO RIGHT WAY TO DO ME WRONG
The Miller Sisters

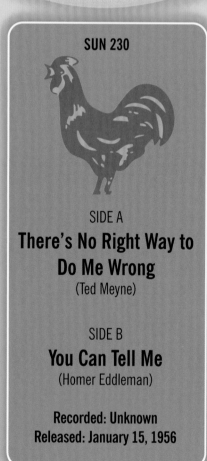

SUN 230

SIDE A
There's No Right Way to Do Me Wrong
(Ted Meyne)

SIDE B
You Can Tell Me
(Homer Eddleman)

Recorded: Unknown
Released: January 15, 1956

The title says it all. The Miller Sisters' treatment matches it: perky, clever, unquestionably country, in this case with close sisterly harmonies that recalled the Davis Sisters' number 1 hit of a couple of years before.

Yes, right in the midst of the birth of the irrepressible new music, just ten days after the release of "Blue Suede Shoes," Sam put out this cute country record, sung by a pair of sisters-in-law, Jo and Millie Miller from Tupelo, Mississippi (the Davis Sisters weren't sisters either), who were managed by Jo's husband, Roy, a guitarist who wrote many of their songs. Inexplicable? Well, yes, kind of—but Sam, as you must understand by now, never wanted to be typed, and not only did he hear something different in the Miller Sisters, he had never entirely given up on his dream—one of his *many* dreams—of establishing a hit country division at Sun, represented here by the bright leads of Sun stalwarts Stan Kesler on steel guitar and Bill Cantrell on fiddle.

The carefully worked-out arrangements and disciplined musicality were undoubtedly the result of rigorous rehearsal under Roy Miller's direction, but most of all it was the Miller Sisters' engagement and charm that came across. I've often wondered if in some part of his mind Sam might not have seen the Miller Sisters' music as the kind that , Becky, a trained singer with a beautiful voice, might have sung had she focused on country rather than pop. But while Becky never made a record (with the exception of her one appearance in the Sun studio for a blues vocal on sax player Johnny London's first, lost session), she was the indispensable link to Sam's "all-girl" radio station, WHER, "1000 watts of beautiful sound," which debuted on October 29, 1955, two months before the Millers Sisters' first Sun release. WHER took its inspiration from the motto of Becky's show, "A smile on your face puts a smile in your voice." Which might very well have been the Miller Sisters' motto, too.

Right: The Miller Sisters.

FOLSOM PRISON BLUES

Johnny Cash and the Tennessee Two

"Folsom Prison Blues" **is perhaps Cash's best known** and most emblematic song, though its authorship is somewhat problematic. (It bears more than a passing resemblance to Gordon Jenkins's "Crescent City Blues," which occasioned a lawsuit and a substantial cash settlement in the '70s.) In any case the song, as modified by Cash, came in many ways to represent the dry, laconic image, leavened by an equally dry sense of humor, that he cultivated over the years, and in fact when he appeared in person at Folsom Prison more than twelve years later (he was by now well on his way to becoming "The Man in Black"), the live album that resulted was the biggest hit of his career. At Folsom he bore down on the line that served most radically to differentiate his version from its original inspiration, shouting out, "I shot a man in Reno / Just to watch him die," as the prison audience, made up of many hard-timers, erupted with cheers and laughter.

The song didn't start out that way. If you check out some of the early takes, you'll discover an almost dirge-like twelve-bar blues, which Sam initially passed over. Then he heard the potential of something else in it. It wasn't just that the song needed to be sped up, he told Cash; he wanted him to completely reimagine it. John might think he had written a song about a prisoner behind bars dreaming of the outside world, but actually he had written something much more universal. Think of it like we're all in prison in a way, Sam said, maybe John should just start thinking about it like that—and then add a beat to it! "That was a part of Sam Phillips's brilliance," Cash reflected in later life. "If the song was there, if he knew the song was there, then he felt at liberty to play with it and doctor it until he had it in that groove that he was hearing in his head. And [then] I started hearing it in my head, [too]."

Left: Johnny inching closer to the full "Man in Back" image.

SUN 232

SIDE A
So Doggone Lonesome
(Cash)

SIDE B
Folsom Prison Blues
(Cash)

Recorded: July 30, 1955
Released: December 3, 1955

THE CHICKEN (DANCE WITH YOU)
Rosco Gordon

Here we have, in a triumphant return to Sun, one of the first artists Sam recorded (even before "Rocket '88'"), one of his earliest hitmakers, and one of his favorite "originals." Sam was taken with Rosco's music from the start. He heard in him not a *good* piano player but a different *kind* of piano player, with a unique, rolling style. "Sam [told me], 'What you're playing, nobody in the world is going to play that but you.' Said, 'I don't know what it is. It's not blues, it's not pop, it's not rock. So we gonna call it "Rosco's Rhythm."' That's what he called it. That's where that came from." And that's what gave Sam his second number 1 R&B hit on Chess, in 1952, with Rosco's grisly humoresque, "Booted."

"The Chicken" was a different matter altogether, a straightforward novelty-dance number, propelled by Rosco's natural high spirits, which, even in the midst of the meteoric rise of "Blue Suede Shoes" on the charts, was a substantial regional hit. Not only that, it resurrected Rosco's career, which would culminate in glorious fashion with his 1960 number-two R&B hit on the Vee-Jay label, "Just a Little Bit," which went on to become a pop and R&B standard.

For "The Chicken," Rosco toured, naturally with a chicken (his name was Butch), and they were quite a hit until Butch died at an early age of alcoholism, perhaps brought on by the reward his owner offered him as an inducement to perform. And though Butch had a successor, Rosco never felt quite the same kinship with him, and by that time, in any case, the record was over.

FLIP/SUN 237

SIDE A
**The Chicken
(Dance with You)**
(Gordon)

SIDE B
Love For You Baby
(Gordon)

Recorded: February 1956
Released: April 25, 1956

Far right: Rosco and Butch the Chicken celebrating the success of "The Chicken" with Sam Phillips.

"The Chicken" was originally the best-selling record on Phillips's Flip label. Phillips re-released it (along with several other Flip singles) on Sun after he discontinued Flip.

ROCK 'N' ROLL RUBY
Warren Smith

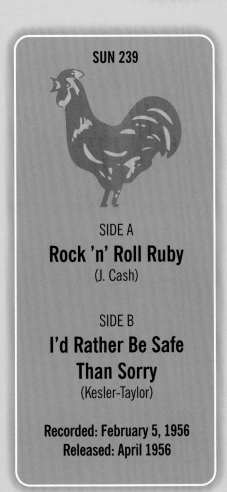

SUN 239

SIDE A
Rock 'n' Roll Ruby
(J. Cash)

SIDE B
I'd Rather Be Safe Than Sorry
(Kesler-Taylor)

Recorded: February 5, 1956
Released: April 1956

Warren Smith was a member of the Snearly Ranch Boys, named for the owner of the boarding house in which the band, including steel guitar player Stan Kesler, all lived. Smith was yet another of those extravagantly gifted, underappreciated talents, who found their way to Sun through the impact of Elvis Presley and yet, for all their gifts, were often plagued with self-doubt.

Warren Smith more than most. "He was the kind of character that needed to be loved a lot," Sam said of Smith. "But a lot of people didn't like him, he perceived that they didn't, and it was his fault in most cases." He didn't much like the song Sam had presented him with either, one that Johnny Cash had written after Sam suggested he could use some good up-tempo material for his rockers. Even with Cash's characteristic good humor and comic word play, everyone agreed it was not one of his most distinguished compositions—and you can't miss the explicit connection to "Blue Suede Shoes." But Smith gave it a great ride anyway, with a strong rhythmic pulse and an easy-going, color-blind, and authentically convincing rockabilly sound. And if, as Sam said, "Warren had a lot of emotional problems," he could declare with equal honesty, "[he was] just interesting enough that I liked him a whole lot."

Left: Warren Smith (center) rocking with Al Hopson (guitar) and Marcus Van Story (bass).

I WALK THE LINE
Johnny Cash

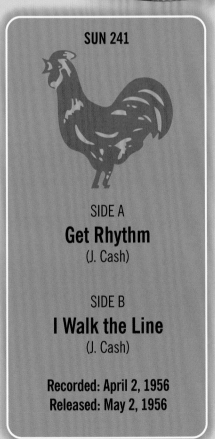

SUN 241

SIDE A
Get Rhythm
(J. Cash)

SIDE B
I Walk the Line
(J. Cash)

Recorded: April 2, 1956
Released: May 2, 1956

Right: April 4, 1957, Memphis. Jerry Lee Lewis's "Whole Lot of Shakin' Going On" won't be released until three weeks into this tour. Carl Perkins hadn't seen a hit in a year. Together with Billy Riley, they were Johnny Cash's supporting acts for a tour that ran from March 31 until mid-May.

Left: Cash performing with the Tennessee Two, Marshall Grant (bass) and Luther Perkins (guitar).

"I Walk the Line" is perhaps the best-known of all of Johnny Cash's songs, and certainly one of his finest compositions. Cash always told the story of how he had come to write it while he was stationed in Germany and became mesmerized by the eerie sound of a guitar that had been recorded by someone else on his Wilcox-Gay tape recorder. After months of trying to figure it out, one day he re-spooled the tape and discovered that it had been on backward and upside down the whole time. After that, the lyrics were relatively easy, and highly personal, but he was still fumbling around for a title when he got into a conversation with Carl Perkins one day about the way of life into which so many had fallen on the road. John declared at that point, perhaps a little wistfully with regard to his own future intentions, "Not me, buddy, I'm walking the line." And Carl told him that was it.

But still, that was not the end of it. The song had started out, like so many of his other songs, as a slow, earnest love ballad with the familiar Johnny Cash and the Tennessee Two boom-chick-a boom-chick-a-boom sound. When Sam suggested that they speed it up a little, John fought him tooth and nail. He just didn't hear it that way, he said. And when in the end he capitulated and recorded a couple of takes at a faster tempo, he did so with the sole intention of shutting Sam up and left the studio convinced that Sam would never be able to bring himself to like that version either.

"The first time I heard it [in its sped-up version] on the radio," Cash said, "I called him and said, 'I hate that sound. Please don't release any more records. I hate that sound.'" But the more he heard it, the more he came to like it. And once the record was an assured pop success (it went to number 1 on the country charts, number 17 on the pop), "Sam said, 'That's what music is all about. It should be universal.' And I said, 'Well, Mr. Phillips, that's what I've always believed too.'"

OOBY DOOBY
Roy Orbison and the Teen Kings

Right: Roy Orbison (sans glasses, in the light suit) with the Teen Kings.

SUN 242

SIDE A
Ooby Dooby
(Penne–Moore)

SIDE B
Go! Go! Go!
(Orbison)

Recorded: March 27, 1956
Released: May 2, 1956

Roy Orbison was yet another Elvis disciple, although in the development of his own music he did not remain one for long. Orbison was a nineteen-year-old college student from Wink, Texas, with deep roots in country music when he first saw Elvis perform in the spring of 1955. He was converted instantly, and not long afterward two fellow students at North Texas State, just as much in Elvis's thrall as Roy himself, wrote a nonsense song called "Ooby Dooby," which quickly became Roy's signature number. (Nonsense songs were, and would continue to be, an integral component of rock 'n' roll—take "Blue Suede Shoes," for example—for the way in which they would always represent a conscious casting-off of the heavy bonds of reason.) Orbison recorded it first for a small Texas label in March 1956, and having been advised by Johnny Cash that if he wanted to make something of himself in the world of music he needed to be on Sun, he gave Sam Phillips a call. Sam's initial reaction was unsurprising. According to Orbison: "He said, 'Johnny Cash doesn't run my record company' and hung up on me." But then, once Sam had heard the record, he suggested that Roy come into his studio and record it properly. Roy did, and Sam bought out the original label, issuing the new version with Roy's own "Go! Go! Go! (Down the Line)," which was very much in the same vein and proved just as enduring.

What impressed Sam most about this new singer, apart from his full-throated vocal range, was his seriousness, even in his approach to a fundamentally silly novelty number. They recorded take after take, but unlike almost any of the other artists Sam had worked with, Black or White, Roy approached every take virtually the same. "Roy was a perfectionist in the best sense," Sam said. "I don't think people generally know how good a guitar player Roy was. His timing would amaze me, with him playing lead and filling in, he would do a lot of combination string stuff, but it was all pushing real good." The difference between the takes was sometimes almost undetectable, but in the end Sam got the sound he wanted.

Along with Carl Perkins, Johnny Cash, and Warren Smith, and with Sonny Burgess and Billy Riley soon to come, Roy instantly took his place in the orbit of Stars Inc., a booking and management office that Sam had just formed with Bob Neal to promote all of Sun's top artists. But, for all of his near-instant success, Roy Orbison from the start wanted to pursue a different path. "Sam Phillips's contribution was to get us to sing with soul," he said, but Roy wanted to sing *ballads* with soul, and very soon he came to feel that he was never going to be given that chance on the Sun label.

OOBY DOOBY
OOBY DOOBY
OOBY DOOBY
OOBY DOOBY
OOBY DOOBY
OOBY DOOBY

OOBY DOOBY
HAS CAUGHT FIRE
by
ROY ORBISON
SUN #242

OOBY DOOBY OOBY DOOBY

OOBY DOOBY

OOBY DOOBY

BOPPIN' THE BLUES/ALL MAMA'S CHILDREN
Carl Perkins

Here are two more versions of the Jimmy DeBerry theme (on "All Mama's Children" it's obvious who's rocking, on "Boppin' the Blues" it's Grandpa who gets rhythm), and two more variations on the nonsense theme. But "Boppin' the Blues" is, certainly, a worthy follow-up to "Blue Suede Shoes," with an even more propulsive boogie-woogie beat and all the surging, hovering-on-the-edge-of rhythmic control that Sam Phillips had picked up in Carl Perkins's delivery from the first.

And yet it didn't hit in anything like the same way as Carl's astonishing debut. In fact, it didn't hit at all. Perhaps this should not be all that surprising. Carl Perkins was nothing like the charismatic performer that Elvis was, and his career was interrupted at the exact moment that it started to take off by a bad automobile accident. And, of course, in the year that followed, Elvis dominated all three charts—pop, country, and rhythm and blues—in a way that left little room for anyone else. Still, even without ever getting that all-important follow-up hit, Carl Perkins continued to display the same triple-threatedness that Chuck Berry alone seemed to possess (listen to the unabashed admiration that Carl, and everyone else, expresses for Berry on the "Million Dollar Quartet" session), as he continued to create a body of work that, much in the manner of Chuck, showcases the kind of antic vocals, striking guitar style, and slyly mischievous lyrics that will forever separate him from the ranks of the also-rans.

SUN 243

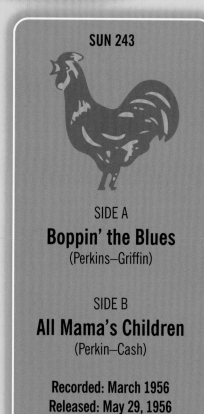

SIDE A
Boppin' the Blues
(Perkins–Griffin)

SIDE B
All Mama's Children
(Perkin–Cash)

Recorded: March 1956
Released: May 29, 1956

Left: Sally Wilbourn, who went to work for Sun as Marion Keisker's assistant on November 21, 1955, and subsequently became Sam Phillips's long-time assistant and companion, holding Carl's now-iconic Dance Album.

Right: Carl Perkins in the movie Jamboree with his brothers Clayton on bass and Jay on rhythm guitar. W. S. Holland is on drums.

TROUBLE BOUND/ ROCK WITH ME BABY
Billy Riley

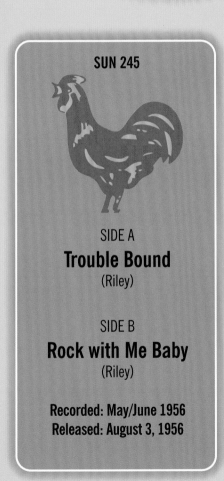

SUN 245

SIDE A
Trouble Bound
(Riley)

SIDE B
Rock with Me Baby
(Riley)

Recorded: May/June 1956
Released: August 3, 1956

Left: Billy Riley studio portrait.

Okay, this may be starting to sound familiar. Guess why Billy Riley, an accomplished twenty-two-year-old country singer from Pocahontas, Arkansas, came to the Sun studio—but, first, listen to how he got there.

Fate once again played a role.

Billy was driving down the highway when who should he encounter but Jack Clement and Jack's employer, truck driver and Fernwood Records owner Slim Wallace, hitchhiking their way back to Memphis. (It's a long story.) By the time they all arrived, Billy was a Fernwood artist, but then when Jack Clement brought the record he cut on Billy to Sam Phillips to have it mastered (almost inexplicably, Sam was still doing mastering, he was even cutting "personal records" like the one he had cut for Elvis three years earlier), Sam picked up on something he liked, both in the record and in the man who had brought it to him. The upshot was that Jack Clement never left. Two weeks later he went to work for Sam as Sun's first outside employee.

Rarely have two such antic, and in many ways antithetical, creative spirits, come together in so fruitful a fashion, arguing and collaborating for the next two years to the advantage of both, and, of course, to the greater glory of Sun. And after Jack left Sun under less than glorious circumstances ("Your services with this company have been terminated," Sam's letter to him began), he went on to become one of Nashville's most beguiling characters, naming himself in highly ironic fashion "Cowboy" Jack Clement (there was no one more uncowboy-like than Jack), and going on to discover, produce, and write songs for Charley Pride, country music's first Black star, and Sam's long-awaited counterpart to Elvis Presley, who would cross over, just as Elvis once had, but going in the opposite direction.

In a way, then, the story of Billy Riley (later to rename himself Billy "Lee" Riley) was as tied in with events as it was with his first Sun record. But "Trouble Bound" is a terrific debut, for all of its echoes of "Heartbreak Hotel," and gives more than a hint of Billy Riley's life-long affinity for the blues, while the other side, "Rock with Me Baby," speaks for itself. Billy was another one of those all-purpose talents that Sam was so drawn to (in an academic setting he would be known as an inspired generalist, something the academy could sorely use), whose talent was almost too great to be bottled up. Which in some ways was the story of his subsequent career.

RED HEADED WOMAN/ WE WANNA BOOGIE
Sonny Burgess

SUN 247

SIDE A
Red Headed Woman
(Burgess)

SIDE B
We Wanna Boogie
(Burgess)

Recorded: May 2, 1956
Released: August 3, 1956

*Right: Sonny's handwritten lyrics for
"Red Headed Woman."*

Left: Sonny in the recording studio.

You could say many of the same things here (check off Elvis, check off musical passions, check off talent and versatility), except in the case of Sonny Burgess the keyword might simply be enthusiasm. Like Billy Riley, Sonny Burgess was one of the preeminent wildmen of Southern rock. (Where Billy swung from the rafters, Sonny and his band, the Pacers, did splits and backflips and jumped into the audience from the stage, or sometimes even the balcony.) One of the highlights of their performance was a dance that they called The Bug, where Sonny would throw a "bug" at one of the guys, who would then, as Sonny described it, "start itching and going crazy, then he'd throw it on somebody else, and we'd throw it all around the audience," after which general madness would ensue. Now, the question you might ask is, how could all this be translated into a studio setting? Sam's answer was simple. "What he wanted [us] to do in that studio was to play like [we] were doing a show," Sonny said. "He thought folks could hear that on the tape. So that's how we did it. We played for Sam. He was our audience, and we tried to impress him the same way we did an audience."

This was Sonny's first record, and when Sam played it back for the group, they begged Sam to let them do it over. But Sam said the mistakes didn't matter, it was the feel that counted. And he was right. Ignore the catastrophic ending. Ignore any out-of-tuneness of voice or instruments (Sam did) and the eleventh commandment that rockabilly shall have no trumpet. As Sam said, "They were a working band [who] knew what they were doing, and they had a sound like I've never heard. Maybe Sonny's sound was too raw, I don't know—but I tell you this. They were pure rock and roll."

COME ON LITTLE MAMA
Ray Harris

SUN 254

SIDE A
Come On Little Mama
(Harris—Cogswell)

SIDE B
**Where'd You Stay
Last Night**
(Harris—Cogswell)

Recorded: June 20, 1956
Released: September 24, 1956

As Sonny Burgess said of so much of the music that they all played, "It just made you feel good. You'd get in that groove, and, man, it made you want to dance if you could[n't] dance a lick, you know, you'd get high just with the music. That was it. Man, you just felt so good it was like you wanted to jump out of your skin." Ray Harris, a Tupelo-area native, may have come into it with less natural aptitude than the others, but he had *exactly* the same attitude. He was working with Bill Black at the Firestone Tire & Rubber plant when Bill invited him to a session with this kid, in fact another Tupelo native, that he and Scotty Moore were working with at Sun. Ray's recollection of just what song they were cutting with Elvis Presley varied in the telling, but his reaction never did. He was determined to do the same thing, create the same excitement, whether or not he had ever sung a lick in his life. He put together a band, and he went home and practiced, and practiced, and practiced. The neighbors got so upset, according to Sun historians Colin Escott and Martin Hawkins, that he had to promise them free copies of the record he was working on if and when it ever came out.

Eventually he came up with something that Sam liked, a song called "Come On Little Mama" that Escott dubbed a pure distillation of "maniacal energy," with limited musicianship, virtually indecipherable lyrics, and a delivery that Sam found irresistible. "I'll never forget it," Sam told Escott, "he was so intense he looked like he was going to have a heart attack every time he played." So buckle up and enjoy the experience—but don't have a heart attack. And don't worry, Ray eventually found a place in the music industry as one of the cofounders, along with Quinton Claunch and Bill Cantrell, of Hi Records, eventual home of Al Green, and in the '70s he became co-owner of a studio in Tupelo with his in-law Sam Phillips (Sam's son Jerry married Ray's daughter Ryta). So you could say everything worked out in the end.

Right: Ray Harris.

I NEED A MAN
Barbara Pittman

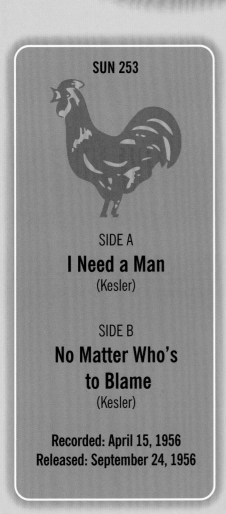

SUN 253

SIDE A
I Need a Man
(Kesler)

SIDE B
**No Matter Who's
to Blame**
(Kesler)

Recorded: April 15, 1956
Released: September 24, 1956

Barbara Pittman presented a not entirely dissimilar case. This was a woman with an immense desire for success. If the talent wasn't all there at the beginning, the determination certainly was. Barbara Pittman had run away with cowboy star and bullwhip performer Lash LaRue's traveling show in her midteens (LaRue was the original "Man in Black"), joined the Snearly Ranch Boys as their "girl singer," and was told by Sam "to go out and learn how to sing" the first time she presented herself at his studio. When she came back after a suitable period of study, she was given the full Sun treatment, with lots of echo, slap bass, and a roughened vocal that started out with "Wellllll" and included plenty of squeals. *Billboard* applauded "the back shack sound, female style" of her Sun debut, and Sam showed his newfound belief in her by recording her for the next four or five years in a number of guises and genres. She found her place in rock history eventually as a prominent figure in the rockabilly revival of the '80s and '90s, one of the few female rockers, along with Wanda Jackson, to make her mark on the music.

Right: Barbara Pittman and Sam Phillips.

Left: Studio portrait of Barbara Pittman.

SWEET AND EASY TO LOVE
Roy Orbison and the Roses

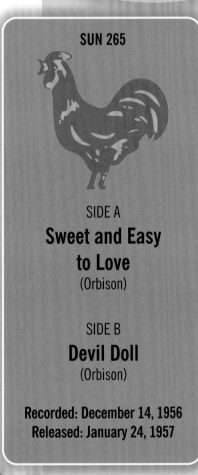

SUN 265

SIDE A
Sweet and Easy to Love
(Orbison)

SIDE B
Devil Doll
(Orbison)

Recorded: December 14, 1956
Released: January 24, 1957

Sam tried one more rocking single with Roy Orbison after "Ooby Dooby" (it was pretty good), then handed him over to Jack Clement to produce, the first artist he allowed Jack to work with on his own. When that failed, Sam let himself be persuaded to try the direction in which Roy really wanted to go, though I'm not sure Sam's heart was really in it. It was a Roy Orbison original, carefully conceived and well-rehearsed, with a perfectly (if generically) executed guitar solo. But even with a heavy back beat and a crooning, Elvis-styled chorus that Roy brought in from Texas, "Sweet and Easy to Love" was, unfortunately, neither here nor there, and it was the last record Sam would produce on Roy, turning him over to Jack Clement for good this time, though Jack was evidently no more convinced than Sam that this new direction was going to work. "Roy always had these crazy ideas," Clement said. "He wanted production numbers like he ultimately wound up doing. I told Roy he'd never make it as a ballad singer. He never let me forget that either.... But me and Roy got to be big buddies [later]."

So why, you might ask, include "Sweet and Easy to Love" at all? Well, that's simple. Because it's a harbinger of the future, Roy believed in it, and it shows how far removed he was from the Sun model, even in his first year on the label. In another year he would be gone for a far brighter future, in which obviously all of his more dramatic aspirations would be realized, and all of Sam Phillips's and Jack Clement's reservations would be proved overwhelmingly wrong.

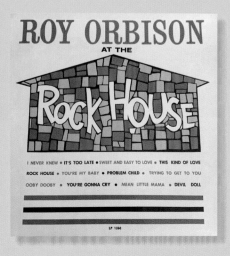

Left: After Orbison achieved success on Monument Records, Phillips overdubbed and repackaged his Sun recordings.

Far left: Orbison, now with glasses (but before the iconic sunglasses), heading out on tour.

"I didn't open the studio to record funerals and weddings and school day revues. I knew what I opened the studio for. I was looking for a higher ground, for what I knew existed in the soul of mankind."

—Sam Phillips

Knox Music, In[.] BMI U-227

Vocal

FEELIN' LOW
(Pee Wee Maddux)
ERNIE CHAFFIN
262

MEMPHIS, TENNESSEE

FEELIN' LOW
Ernie Chaffin

And yet it can't be said that Sam had anything against ballads, per se.

Ernie Chaffin was one of the few artists to arrive at the Sun studio fully formed. And he definitely wasn't influenced by Elvis. He was thirty-eight years old, lived in Gulfport, Mississippi, and had made several records already. He arrived with his own band, his own songs, and a style and direction all his own. The music that he was drawn to could best be described as "heart music," the kind of music that Eddy Arnold made at the start of his career with songs like "Many Tears Ago." But Chaffin brought a unique twist to that easy-going style, which Sam immediately responded to. "Feelin' Low" comes across, like many of Don Gibson's songs, and some of Charlie Rich's too, as a pop number that does not shrink from heartbreak. "We had a kind of beat on that thing that was very interesting," Sam told Sun historian Martin Hawkins. "It was an upbeat—I don't mean up-tempo—and offbeat lick on the thing that made it very fine."

Right: Ernie Chaffin, not looking like he's feelin' too low.

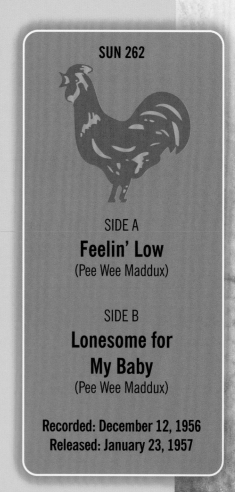

SUN 262

SIDE A
Feelin' Low
(Pee Wee Maddux)

SIDE B
Lonesome for My Baby
(Pee Wee Maddux)

Recorded: December 12, 1956
Released: January 23, 1957

Vocal
U-229

BMI

CRAZY ARMS
(Seals-R. Mdooney)
JERRY LEE LEWIS
With His
Pumping Piano
259
MEMPHIS, TENNESSEE

CRAZY ARMS
Jerry Lee Lewis with His Pumping Piano

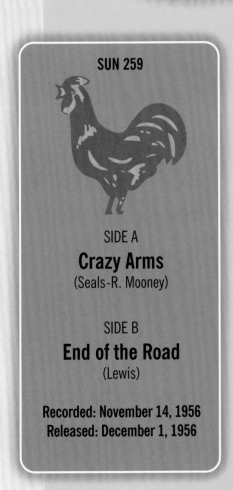

SUN 259

SIDE A
Crazy Arms
(Seals-R. Mooney)

SIDE B
End of the Road
(Lewis)

Recorded: November 14, 1956
Released: December 1, 1956

Left: Jerry Lee Lewis—
the look for '57.

Okay, remember I said, "This is it," I'm sure more than once? Well, this was definitely it once again, a pivotal moment in the history of rock 'n' roll. Maybe even a pivotal moment in the history of music. It might have seemed liked it happened by accident, but it didn't. It was propelled by the sheer determination of one man who had come to claim his destiny. Twenty-one-year-old Jerry Lee Lewis had read a magazine story about Elvis that cited Sam Phillips as the guiding influence behind all these rising stars—Elvis, Johnny Cash, Carl Perkins, even B. B. King—and, because he saw himself as no less a talent than any of the others, he said to his father, "This is the man we need to go see."

Jerry Lee and his father, Elmo, arrived in Memphis, having sold all the eggs from their little farm in Ferriday, Louisiana, to make the trip. Sam wasn't there, but Jack Clement was. Jerry Lee ran through as much of his wide-ranging repertoire as he could—blues, country, boogie woogie, and rock 'n' roll—all played on the piano in a style unlike anything Jack (or anyone else) had ever heard. When Sam came back and Jack played him the tape, "I said, 'Where in hell did this man come from?' I mean, he played that piano with *abandon*." But that wasn't all; others might do that just as well. "Between the stuff he played and didn't play," Sam said, "I could hear that spiritual thing, too. I told Jack, 'Just get him in here as fast as you can.'"

The first single came about with the same kind of serendipity. Jerry Lee was playing one of his current favorites, Ray Price's "Crazy Arms," which had been number 1 on the country charts for nearly half the year and was currently number 2, with just eighteen-year-old drummer J. M. Van Eaton accompanying him. (Both the guitarist and the bass player were out of the room right up until the very last chord.) So incendiary was his style, so original his approach that Sam unhesitatingly chose it as his first single, saying he didn't care how big Ray Price's version was, this was a certifiable *hit*.

And he was right. It worked in a way that few other debuts, with the exception of Elvis's, have ever worked. But it's what came next, as a result of that first record's success (*see p. 172*), that would really turn the world on its head. As Jerry Lee Lewis said years later, speaking of himself and Sam and Jack Clement, "Nutty as a fox squirrel. Birds of a feather flock together. It took all of us to get together to really screw up the world. We've done it!"

Knox Music, In[c]
BMI U-231

Vocal

MATCHBOX
(Perkins)
CARL PERKINS
261
MEMPHIS, TENNESSEE

MATCHBOX
Carl Perkins

This might well be as rocking as Carl Perkins "The Rockin' Guitar Man" ever got. With a just-arrived-in-Memphis Jerry Lee Lewis on piano, "Matchbox" just *churns*. It probably should be stated that Carl Perkins was not altogether satisfied with the sparks that were flying from the piano keys. "I mean, Jerry Lee played the piano like he wanted to play it, and you didn't tell him—if he didn't want to play it the way you wanted to, he'd say, 'Well, there it sits. *You* play it.'" But I don't think there's any question that Carl knew they were getting something rare and unrepeatable. And who knows what they might have come up with next? Maybe the only way they could have topped "Matchbox" would have been if they had gone on to record Sister Rosetta Tharpe's jumping gospel standard, "Strange Things Happening Every Day," a musical bedrock not just for Carl and Jerry Lee but for Elvis and Johnny Cash, too. But it's a moot point. Whatever else they might have had in mind, fate intervened in the person of Elvis Presley, whose arrival brought Carl's session to an abrupt halt, after which the Million Dollar Quartet took place.

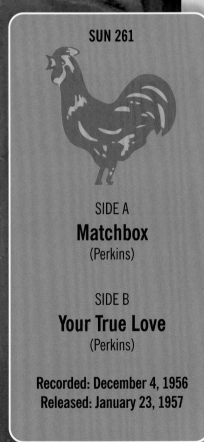
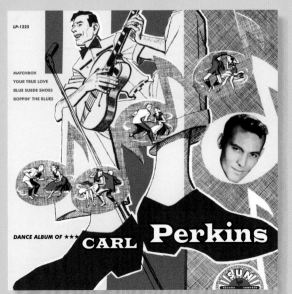

Left: The original "best of," the Dance Album.

Far left: Carl Perkins at Overton Park Shell, Memphis, June 1, 1956. His brother, Jay, is in a neck brace following their car wreck on March 22.

FLYIN' SAUCERS ROCK & ROLL

Billy Riley and His Little Green Men

Well, you know, maybe a little foolish (flying saucers and all that), but you can't deny that it does epitomize in many ways the spirit of rock 'n' roll. By now, with Sam's and Jack's help, Billy had put together a band made up principally of guitarist Roland Janes and drummer J. M. Van Eaton, a recent high school graduate, who from this point on would together become the backbone of the Sun studio sound.

In this case, they all clicked right away, with Jerry Lee once again on piano, on a weightless kind of atomic-age thing that Roland had brought in. After a couple of takes, Sam said they were doing just fine, but it felt like they needed to sound a little bit more like they came from outer space. That's when Roland kicked it off with his whammy bar, while Jerry Lee contributed a steady, rumbling undercurrent, and bass player Marvin Pepper screamed loud vocal encouragement. As soon as Sam heard it, Billy said, "he just jumped straight up and said 'Man that's it. You sound like a bunch of little green men from Mars!' He said, 'That'd be a good name for this band, The Little Green Men. That's what we'll put on the record.'"

SUN 260

SIDE A
Flyin' Saucers Rock & Roll
(Ray Scott)

SIDE B
I Want You Baby
(Billy Riley)

Recorded: December 11, 1956
Released: February 1, 1957

Right: Billy Riley with the second generation of Little Green Men. From left: Martin Willis, Pat O'Neill, Riley, Jimmy Wilson, J. M. Van Eaton.

WHOLE LOT OF SHAKIN' GOING ON
Jerry Lee Lewis

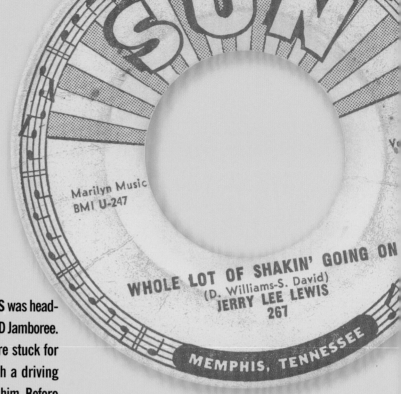

Not long after the release of his first record, **Jerry Lee Lewis** was heading for Dallas with Roland Janes and J. M. Van Eaton for an appearance on the Big D Jamboree. Along the way they stopped to play a show in Blytheville, Arkansas, and were stuck for material on what turned out to be a four-hour gig. Jerry Lee came up with a driving boogie-woogie number he used to sing in Ferriday, and the band fell in behind him. Before he had even gotten halfway through, Roland said, the people just started going crazy, "bopping all over the floor, you know how they do in Arkansas." And as soon as they finished, the audience wanted to hear it again. "Play that 'Shakin' song," they kept calling out. "They just loved it, man," Roland said. "They insisted on hearing it over and over." The same thing happened when they played the Big D the next night. "So we all agreed," Roland said, "as soon as we get back to Memphis we need to go and see if Sam will let us cut it. That's a dandy."

That's what they did. "Whole Lot of Shakin' Going On" didn't come as easy as "Crazy Arms" had, but it came—and it came even better. It was released at the end of April 1957, but it took a full three months for the record to build, and then only through the promotional genius of Sam's brother Jud, who had rejoined the company, after an absence of three years, due solely to his belief in Jerry Lee Lewis's talent. He took Jerry to New York to get him on national TV and, without a single appointment in advance or any press write-ups or anything but his invincible salesman's charm and determination to make his case, got him an audition for the *Steve Allen Show*. "The [producer]," recalled Jerry Lee, "looked at Jud like he was crazy. I just sat there blowing bubblegum. This guy looked at me, and I looked at him. Finally he said, 'Okay, kid, let's see you play piano and sing.' I walked over to the piano, and this guy sat down and put his feet up on his desk like he was going to get a big laugh. The minute I started in on 'Whole Lot of Shakin', this guy came up out of his chair and got down behind me and just crouched down looking over my shoulder the whole time I was playing. When I finished, he said to Jud, 'I'll give you $500 if you don't show him to anyone else. And bring him back first thing Monday morning. I want Steve to hear him.'"

His appearance, on July 28, 1957, was nothing short of cataclysmic. If you don't believe me, watch the video. And now watch it again. And again. It is, unquestionably, one of the defining moments of rock 'n' roll, as Jerry Lee kicks out the piano stool, and Steve Allen sends it flying back. But it was all just in a day's work for Jerry Lee Lewis, and the record went on to top the country and R&B charts, falling just short in the pop field, where in one of the great miscarriages of musical justice it was eclipsed by Canadian teenager Paul Anka's saccharine "Diana" and film actor Debbie Reynolds's even more saccharine "Tammy."

SUN 267

SIDE A
**Whole Lot of Shakin'
Going On**
(D. Williams—S. David)

SIDE B
It'll Be Me
(Jack Clement)

Recorded: February 1957
Released: April 24, 1957

*Right: Jerry Lee Lewis with dee-jay/
presenter Art Laboe in the background.
El Monte Legion Stadium, 1958.*

Inset: Jerry Lee's first LP.

Jerry Lee Lewis

Don't Be Cruel
Goodnight Irene
Put Me Down
It All Depends
Ubangi Stomp
Crazy Arms

Jambalaya
Fools Like Me
High School Confidential
When The Saints
Go Marching In
Matchbox
It'll Be Me

MISS FROGGIE/ SO LONG I'M GONE
Warren Smith

SUN 268

SIDE A
So Long I'm Gone
(Roy Orbison)

SIDE B
Miss Froggie
(W. Smith)

Recorded: January/
February 1957
Released: April 15, 1957

Here we get a wild blues mélange by Warren Smith backed by an appealing country shuffle (written by Roy Orbison), once again showing both the versatility and immoderacy of Warren Smith's talent. "Miss Froggie" was certainly the more calculated effort from an artist who considered himself first and foremost a country singer, but here he proves no less adept, and no less an agent of spontaneity, at rocking the blues. Listen to the solid rhythmic underpinning and feeling he puts into such fundamentally frivolous lyrics. Then turn the record over and get a glimpse of what the future holds in store for Smith, presaging the brief string of Top 40 country hits he would have on the Liberty label in the '60s.

Right: Warren Smith and Sam Phillips.

Left: Studio portrait of Warren Smith.

RED HOT
Billy Riley and His Little Green Men

As promised, here comes another one of Billy "The Kid" Emerson's signature songs roaring back to life in a raucous new rockabilly version by Billy Riley and His Little Green Men. You might say it's nowhere near as cool as Billy "The Kid"'s original, but it definitely serves its own supercharged purpose, offering a template for every true rockabilly to show up over the next fifty or sixty years. Bob Dylan endorsed the Billy Riley version. "Billy's hit song was called 'Red Hot,'" he said, "and it was red hot. It could blast you out of your skull and make you feel happy about it." And who could argue with that? And it's certainly true: whatever the relative merits of each version, this wide-open, full-throttle approach instantly became, as Dylan said, an almost eponymous evocation of the way music is supposed to make you feel.

Left: The Little Green Men getting red hot.

SUN 277

SIDE A
Red Hot
(Emerson)

SIDE B
Pearly Lee
(Billy Riley)

Recorded: January 30, 1957
Released: September 14, 1957

GIVE MY LOVE TO ROSE/ HOME OF THE BLUES

Johnny Cash and the Tennessee Two

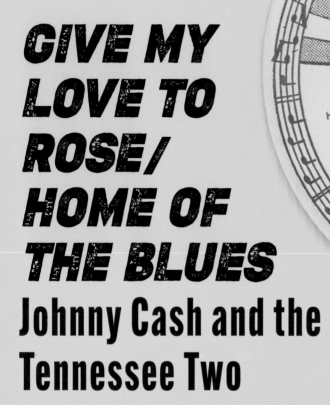

Sam Phillips considered Johnny Cash one of his greatest artists both because of the simplicity of his technique and the eloquence of his message. It's hard to say what Cash will be most remembered for—his voice, his originality, his songwriting, or simply his presence. What Sam admired him for most, though, apart from that inimitable voice (the one voice, Sam said, that challenged Howlin' Wolf for instant recognition), was his songwriting skill, his ability to tell a story or create a mood with the minimalism of an Ernest Hemingway or Raymond Carver short story.

Both of these songs come from the July 1957 session at which Jack Clement for the first time was given the opportunity to work with Cash on his own. With "Home of the Blues," John said, he was striving for some of the purity that he had recently found in folklorist Alan Lomax's blues field recordings and, while Jack's busy overdubs get in the way sometimes (after all, this *was* his first big opportunity), the song's never-less-than-caustic lyrics achieve some of that aim.

But for me, "Give My Love to Rose," patterned loosely after a popular western folk song recorded in the 1920s, comes much closer to the spirit of the blues. It's a tale told by a dying hobo to an unidentified narrator, who vanishes after the first verse. What is so remarkable about the song is the way it frames an entire life in just a few short verses, as the chorus ("Give my love to Rose / Please won't you, mister") brings the listener up short every time. Listen to the forlorn opening notes of the guitar, listen to Cash's voice, as desolate and unadorned as you'll ever hear it—it just always gets me. See if it doesn't get you, too.

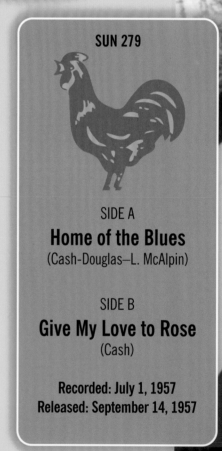

SUN 279

SIDE A
Home of the Blues
(Cash-Douglas—L. McAlpin)

SIDE B
Give My Love to Rose
(Cash)

Recorded: July 1, 1957
Released: September 14, 1957

Right: Cash with the Tennessee Two.

Inset: Cash's fifth EP for Sun,
Home of the Blues.

SEP 116

Johnny Cash

Image TK

HOME OF THE BLUES

- YOU'RE THE NEAREST THING TO HEAVEN
- I CAN'T HELP IT
- HOME OF THE BLUES
- BIG RIVER

SUN

d and first

U-277
Vocal
1:50

GREAT BALLS OF FIRE
(Hammer–Blackwell)
JERRY LEE LEWIS
And His Pumping Piano
281
MEMPHIS, TENNESSEE

GREAT BALLS OF FIRE/ YOU WIN AGAIN
Jerry Lee Lewis and His Pumping Piano

How do you follow up an explosive hit like "Whole Lot of Shakin' Going On" (*see p. 172*) with something just as explosive? Generally speaking, you wouldn't even try. But this is Jerry Lee Lewis, and even though it would be impossible to replicate the parthenogenesis of a song like "Whole Lot of Shakin' Going On," Sam Phillips and Jerry Lee Lewis were certainly determined to do their best.

Their methodology in this case came down to one thing: trust your damn instincts.

In the fall of 1957 Jerry Lee was scheduled to make his movie debut in a rock 'n' roll "exploitation" movie called *Jamboree*. Through Hill and Range, the song publishers with whom Sam had established a short-term deal to promote the songs in his publishing catalogue (in other words, almost all the songs recorded by his artists on Sun) in both cover versions and foreign markets, Sam was presented with a song called "Great Balls of Fire," which had been written by Otis Blackwell. Blackwell had been known primarily as a journeyman R&B singer until, in the past year, he had written two of Elvis's biggest hits, "Don't Be Cruel" and "All Shook Up." When Sam first heard the new song, he knew it was perfect for Jerry, and not surprisingly (though Jerry Lee Lewis could never be said to be a go-along guy, he was a keen spotter of talent) Jerry did, too.

They went into the studio in early September to cut the track for the movie and after nine takes got an acceptable master. But both Sam and Jerry Lee were once again in agreement: this was not an acceptable master for release on Sun. So they returned to the studio a few weeks later to try to get it right, the stop-time introduction in particular, which required precision and discipline on everyone's part. The way Sam saw it, you couldn't just "tinker your way into it. 'Great Balls of Fire' is one of those songs that has to be right on the front end or the song won't mean [a thing]. I think it was the toughest song to start that I ever tried to record. We worked our ass off, because those breaks had to be exactly synched with his voice."

In the end, though there was at least one additional instrument in the room, it came down to just voice, piano, and drums, augmented by a lavish application of slapback, and they emerged with something that in anyone else's hands would have been little more than an exuberant novelty number but, in Jerry Lee's and Sam's, emerged as yet another indisputable triumph of energy and belief.

And that barely leaves room to talk about the B-side, "You Win Again," another indisputable masterpiece, as pure an interpretation and transformation of a Hank Williams classic as you will ever find.

SUN 281

SIDE A
Great Balls of Fire
(Hammer–Blackwell)

SIDE B
You Win Again
(Hank Williams)

Recorded: October 8, 1957
Released: November 3, 1957

Left: Jerry Lee pumping the piano for his fans.

Inset: Sam Phillips's self-designed ad for the release of "Great Balls of Fire."

BALLAD OF A TEENAGE QUEEN/ BIG RIVER

Johnny Cash and the Tennessee Two

SUN 283

SIDE A
Ballad of a Teenage Queen
(Clement)

SIDE B
Big River
(Cash)

Recorded: November 12, 1957
Released: December 1957

What are we to make of "Ballad of a Teenage Queen," a silly little ditty, as its author Jack Clement often described it, which, along with "Guess Things Happen That Way" (*see p. 186*), became Johnny Cash's biggest-selling hit on Sun. I suppose you could consider it a sly take-off on Chuck Berry's classic "Johnny B. Goode," in which it's the girl this time who succeeds in Hollywood but, in a reversal that might be taken as either sexist or satirical, or both, turns her back on fame and returns home to marry the boy next door, the one who "worked at the candy store." It seems ironic, doesn't it, that this should have been Cash's biggest commercial success on Sun, for all of the many sober and serious messages he had already delivered—I mean, it's so *insipid*, as Jack would have been the first to agree. But then in more recent years I have heard the song presented in an entirely different, almost elegiac fashion—by both Marty Stuart (with Jack) and John Prine—that seems to cast serious doubt on the story that is being told. So I wonder sometimes—but I'm not going to impose my wonder on you.

Of the other side, though, there can be no doubt. "Big River" incorporated all of the elements that had distinguished Cash's songwriting from the start—wit, conviction, and striking lyrical originality, with a strong suggestion of his deep-seated roots in the "folk" tradition—but it possessed as well the kind of illimitable ambition (was all that clever wordplay merely entertaining, or did it intensify feelings of loss and alienation, as it would one day in the songs of one of Cash's keenest students, Bob Dylan?) that few other Sun artists could suggest. Once again, Jack Clement was the producer, and he played acoustic guitar and bass drum on this song, with the Tennessee Two relegated to a more secondary role. I don't think there's a better Jack Clement production, or a better Johnny Cash record, than this one.

Right: Sun's Canadian licensee, Quality Records, ran "Teenage Queen" contests in conjunction with Johnny Cash's western Canadian tour in 1957. Here, Johnny poses with one of the winners.

Left: A rare color shot of Johnny Cash and the Tennessee Two in the Sun studio.

BREATHLESS
Jerry Lee Lewis and His Pumping Piano

Once again Otis Blackwell came up with the song, and Sam's brother Jud, now Jerry's manager, came up with the sales campaign, though at this point it's doubtful that Jerry Lee really needed it. This would be Jerry Lee's third straight all-categories "Top 7" hit, to be strictly accurate (though I think it really was more like Top 2 or 3 across the board), and like "Great Balls of Fire" it all hinged on a hook that, without the commitment that Jerry Lee (and Sam) brought to it, could have come across as little more than a parodic declaration of passion.

"Breathless" hit the market with as much impact as the previous two singles. Jerry debuted it on the brand-new Saturday-night *Dick Clark Show* on the ABC network, which was a coup in itself, and he played it live, which was a double coup, since everyone else on the show was required to lip-synch. The show, however, had been forced to go on the air without a sponsor. Not a single company, Clark told Jud Phillips, had been willing to step up. Despite the overwhelming success of his daytime show, *American Bandstand*, they were all concerned that rock 'n' roll would not be able to attract a prime-time audience.

As it turned out, the ratings were so good that, by the third show, Beech-Nut had signed on, with the specific aim of promoting their brand-new "flavorific" Spearmint gum to their target audience of teens. That was when Jud came up with his big idea. Why not, he suggested to Clark, leaping blithely into previously uncharted territory, tie in a promotion of Jerry Lee's new record with the gum? It was, he said, a perfect fit. Jerry even chewed Beech-Nut gum. Clark could simply bring him back for a command return performance, and Sun would offer signed copies of the record "free" for just five Beech-Nut gum wrappers plus fifty cents postage and handling.

And that's just what happened.

The promotion was a runaway success, so much so that Sam had to hire an outside staff and train them to package the records in the back of the building. Soon every square inch of studio space was taken over by the task so long as there wasn't a session scheduled, and anyone who wasn't doing something else was recruited for the effort. In the end, thirty-eight thousand copies of the record were shipped out of Memphis, but it went on and on, said Sally Wilbourn, Sam's new assistant, long after they had been forced to let the extra help go.

And the song itself, much like its immediate predecessor, "Great Balls of Fire," was yet another triumphant example of Jerry Lee Lewis's (and Sam's) whole-hearted commitment to the moment and his determination to wring every last element of energy and entertainment, and humor, from every song that he chose to undertake. Others might have dismissed "Breathless" as trivial—but there was no such word in Sam's or Jerry's vocabulary. If you did something, you went all out, and you'd better have fun doing it. And it's clear at every moment in his delivery of this song that Jerry Lee Lewis was having fun. How could anyone fail to be won over by the unrestrained relish with which he embraces the song's title at the end of each verse and then, with even more emphatic insistence at the record's conclusion. "You leave me, ahhhhhh, breathless—uh!" Yes, indeed.

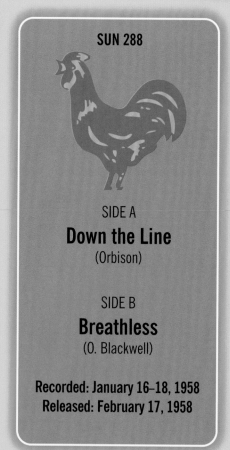

SUN 288

SIDE A
Down the Line
(Orbison)

SIDE B
Breathless
(O. Blackwell)

Recorded: January 16–18, 1958
Released: February 17, 1958

Right: Leaving the crowd breathless.

Inset: Beech-Nut jumping on the rock 'n' roll—and Jerry Lee Lewis—bandwagon.

J-291
Vocal
2:39
a DICK CLARK
Beech-Nut Spearmint Special
SUN
BREATHLESS
JERRY LEE LEWIS
BEECH-NUT GUM
SPEARMINT
it's FLAVOR-IFIC

GUESS THINGS HAPPEN THAT WAY

Johnny Cash and the Tennessee Two

This gets my vote for Jack Clement's finest composition (see page 183 for J. R. Cash's), a wry, shrug-of-the-shoulders acceptance of Things As They Are, which is as much a characteristic of Jack's humor as it is of his philosophy. Unlike "Ballad of a Teenage Queen" (which you'll have to seek out in both of its more melancholy versions), you'll never get tired of listening to this song. With Johnny Cash's flat, equally shoulder-shrugging delivery, it has to be ranked as one of Sun's most existential rock 'n' roll offerings.

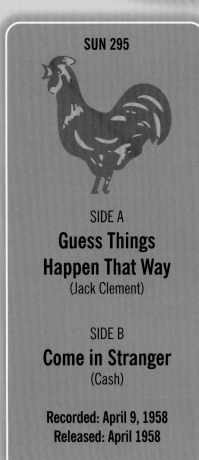

SUN 295

SIDE A

Guess Things Happen That Way

(Jack Clement)

SIDE B

Come in Stranger

(Cash)

Recorded: April 9, 1958
Released: April 1958

Left: One of Johnny's rare Sun EPs, featuring "Guess Things Happen That Way."

Right: Johnny taking a much-needed break.

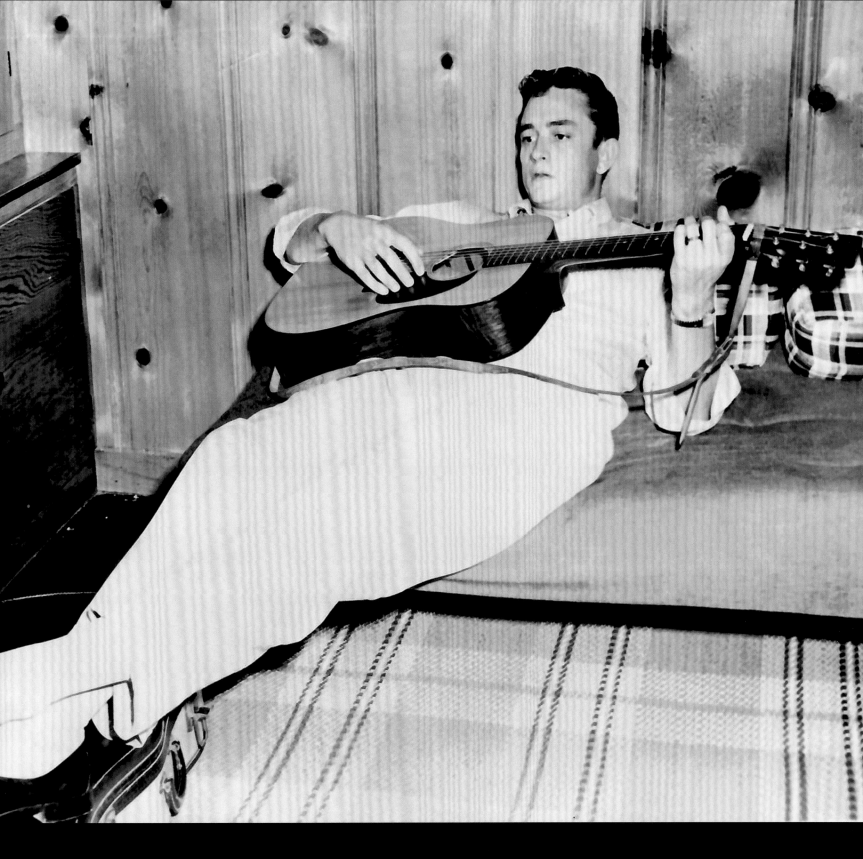

RC KI PD

MEMPHIS TENN 1031P SEP 24 195?

DEWEY "STONE" PHILLIPS

WBBQ MFS

WEBSTERS INTERNATIONAL UNABRIDGED DICTIONARY RAUNCHY MEANS

CLUMSY HARVARDS INDEX DEPT CONCURS

LIBRARIAN "STONE" CITY MEMPHIS COSSITT

1110P ////

RAUNCHY
Bill Justis and His Orchestra

Bill Justis was hired, not too long after Jack Clement, to serve as arranger, producer, saxophone player, and all-around hipster. Up until then he had expressed nothing but the jazz snob's scorn for rock 'n' roll, which he dismissed as the new barbarism ("Strictly squaresville, girls," he might have said to the trained musicians in his big-band society orchestra), but he had been converted by a simple awakening to the opportunity that democracy and capitalism provided to even the unwashed and unskilled.

When, in the fall of 1957, Sam launched a new label, Phillips International, to offer "a wide variety of music, including standard pop and jazz," with every artist prescriptively possessing, the Phillips brochure announced, his own "individual 'sound'—a production element which Sam Phillips personally and constantly looks for, produces, and insists upon in any record," it was only natural that he should offer his new Musical Director the opportunity to make his recording debut. What Bill came up with was not entirely what might have been expected. It came about after an epic late-night drinking session. "It was about three o'clock in the morning," Jack Clement recalled, "everybody was stewed, and we were about to quit." Then Bill said he had this thing he'd been doing in the clubs, and because his regular saxophone player was sick, Bill took the part. Which may have been the reason, as Justis suggested, that the whole thing was so "off-tone, I was [so] out-of-shape on the sax, but I think that was what helped to sell it."

Sam was knocked out when he heard the song for the first time. "My God," he said, "it just blew me away. [Just] three chords in it, like most of my stuff. That's all I wanted. That's enough." What was it called? he asked Justis. Its working title was "Raunchy," Bill said, explaining that when they had got done playing it, he had said to the fellows, "sort of kiddingly, 'Well, that sounded real raunchy.'" So that was what he thought he'd call it. Sam didn't bat an eye about a title that he knew would invite a lot of controversy over a word with explicit (and somewhat seamy) sexual connotations. In fact, he got kind of a kick out of it. That's it, he said emphatically. Bad connotations or not, "that's exactly what that record is!"

And while he did indeed get plenty of blowback, both from DJs, distributors, and the general public (even Dewey Phillips expressed concern), the record took off from the beginning, drawing big-selling pop and R&B covers and reaching number 2 on the pop charts itself. Sam seemed to relish all the criticism. He launched full-page ads in the trades, implored DJs to just "LISTEN," and announced, as if it needed to be said, "We at Phillips International and Sun Records have always tried to create, never copy." Sam even looked the word up in the dictionary and in one of a series of telegrams to his "blood brother" Dewey, declared, "[In] Webster's International Unabridged Dictionary raunchy means clumsy. Harvard's index department concurs [Signed] Librarian 'Stone' City Memphis Cossitt." Cossitt, for those not in the Memphis know, being Memphis's main public library.

And, as a not altogether irrelevant footnote, if you visit the still-very-much-in-business Sam C. Phillips Recording Studio in Memphis, you will see the opening notes of "Raunchy" painted gaily on the transom above the door.

Phillips International 3519

SIDE A
Raunchy
(Justis–Manker)

SIDE B
The Midnite Man
(Justis–Manker)

Recorded: June 5, 1957
Released: September 1957

Left: Bill Justis's background was playing for un-raunchy high society dances.

Inset: A telegram to Dewey Phillips, attempting to allay his fears about the using the word "raunchy."

LONELY WEEKENDS/ EVERYTHING I DO IS WRONG
Charlie Rich

Phillips International 3552

SIDE A
Lonely Weekends
(Rich)

SIDE B
Everything I Do Is Wrong
(Rich)

Recorded: October 14, 1959
Released: January 1960

Right: Charlie Rich.

Charlie Rich came to Sun to begin with not as an artist but as a song-writer and session player. Actually, his wife, Margaret Ann, brought in a tape of some of his songs and presented them to Bill Justis, who admired his jazz-and-blues piano playing but told Margaret Ann he would have to learn to play less technically well, as "bad," in other words, but with as much raw feeling, as some of the other Sun artists.

Charlie set about the task and was soon hired. I should stress that Charlie was a *great* piano player, and much admired by nearly every one of the Sun artists, including Jerry Lee Lewis, with whom Charlie formed a life-long mutual admiration society. Sam was partic-ularly struck by the originality of this new talent and even put out a couple of desultory records that neither one of them much believed in, then encouraged Charlie to write a song for himself that expressed some of the musical feeling that he was putting into the songs he was writing for others. Charlie, a very modest, actually agoraphobic man who was definitely not looking for stardom ("Modesty, modesty," Sam joked, looking back on the experience. "I wanted to slap him sometimes, but he was a big, handsome man, and I was afraid I might get my butt kicked!"), did not take Sam's advice, and the next song he brought to Sam, "Lonely Weekends," was, really, written for Jerry Lee Lewis. Unlike a lot of similar-themed songs of this sort, though, it hid a melancholy message behind a bright, up-tempo exterior, and when Sam heard it, he insisted that Charlie cut it himself.

"Lonely Weekends" was released on Phillips International at the beginning of 1960, with a jaunty "bad luck" blues on the other side, and went to number 22 on the pop charts, which even merited an appearance on Dick Clark's *American Bandstand*. For Charlie, though, the most exciting thing to come out of this brief encounter with fame was when he flew to New York to talk to Clark about going out on national tour and wandered into a little jazz club in the Village. "We just walked in off the street, and there was Mabel Mercer [a legendary but little-known British expatriate and Frank Sinatra inspiration]. I can't really describe it, just her and a piano player—it was one of the grooviest things in the world, just so cool. No, we didn't do [the tour]. God, she was outasight."

IN THE MOOD
The Hawk

Even in the doldrumest of doldrums Sam never gave up on Jerry Lee Lewis, whose career had come completely untracked after a 1958 British tour on which Jerry Lee unapologetically introduced his thirteen-year-old cousin and new wife, Myra, to the press. The English sent him home, his current single, "High School Confidential," well on its way to chart success, was stopped dead in its tracks, his asking price went from $10,000 a night to $250 a night, and he didn't have another hit for three years (*see "What'd I Say" p. 196*). Sam tried everything he could think of to restore the fans' faith (he didn't have to worry about Jerry's faith in himself), but releasing a piano solo on the Phillips label in August of 1960, and crediting it to "The Hawk," probably did not come under the heading of commercial calculation. This was, rather, just one more statement of Sam's belief in Jerry's genius.

I'm sure he took real delight in Jerry Lee's choice of material here. Sam, after all, had started out engineering the big-band broadcasts from the Skyway Ballroom at the Hotel Peabody on his first radio job in Memphis, and he had a great appreciation for the music. He always pointed to Tommy Dorsey's "Boogie Woogie" as one of the early prototypes for rock 'n' roll. And every band that played the Skyway was almost certainly going to play the perennial Glenn Miller favorite, "In the Mood," to which Jerry Lee applies his own irrepressible boogie-woogie interpretation here.

"He was the most talented man I ever worked with, Black or White," Sam once said. "One of the most talented human beings to walk on God's earth. There's not one-millionth of an inch difference [between] the way Jerry Lee Lewis thinks about his music and the way Bach or Beethoven felt about [theirs]."

Right: The Killer, killing it in the rock 'n' roll movie Jamboree *(1957).*

Phillips International 3559

SIDE A
In the Mood
(Razaf–Garland)

SIDE B
I Get the Blues When It Rains
(Klauser–Stoddard)

Recorded: January 21, 1960
Released: August 1960

TELEPHONE

ONE

Knox Music
Inc., BMI

SAM C

SAM C

the webbs

WHO WILL THE NEXT FOOL BE
Charlie Rich

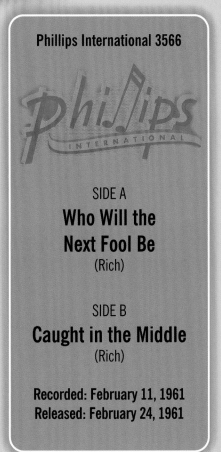

Phillips International 3566

SIDE A
**Who Will the
Next Fool Be**
(Rich)

SIDE B
Caught in the Middle
(Rich)

Recorded: February 11, 1961
Released: February 24, 1961

*Left: Charlie Rich in a publicity
shot from 1960.*

Of all his artists, Sam saw Charlie Rich alone as standing on the same level of emotional profundity as Howlin' Wolf. It was a point he never failed to make, no matter what the subject of the interview, despite the vast differences between the two in background and style. But if he felt he had done all he could to bring out the underlying greatness of Howlin' Wolf's music, he never felt he had done the same for Charlie Rich, whether as a blues singer or as a sophisticated jazz musician. Somehow Charlie eluded him. The pain that he felt, the sense that Sam had that his very nerve endings were exposed, rarely expressed itself without some form of disguise in the studio.

But here it does.

"Who Will the Next Fool Be" was one of the inaugural recordings at Sam's new studio in Nashville (see p. 45), whose first employee, Billy Sherrill, was the architect of the lushly orchestrated "Nashville sound" of the '70s and '80s that finally established Charlie Rich as a superstar ("Behind Closed Doors, "The Most Beautiful Girl"), then led him to virtually quit the business. It is a song that for the first time expresses some of the wellsprings of emotion that lie at the heart of Charlie's music, modulated by the edge of a self-consciously-created hip sensibility. "After you get rid of me / Who will the next fool be?" he sang, lagging behind the beat and then, as the song progressed, showing off those little curlicues of style, breaking meter, throwing in swoops of unexpected emphasis, reaching for the high, vaulting notes at the top of his range. For once, Sam felt he had gotten him untracked and enabled Charlie to display some of the depth of feeling that placed him in that same strange, uncategorizable category as the Howlin' Wolf.

Just as a postscript, while Charlie Rich's 1961 release never appeared on the pop charts, Bobby "Blue" Bland's elegiac, and very soulful, version (listen not just to Bobby's thrilling vocal but to bandleader Joe Scott's perfectly calibrated arrangement) went to number 12 on the R&B chart the following year, a rare instance in which the same, deeply personal pop song generates two incomparable masterpieces. (Or maybe not so rare—think of "Mystery Train" and "That's All Right," though here the sources are clearly not so personal.) Just to keep the record straight, I wouldn't even try to choose between the two.

Finally, as something much more than a postscript, it should be noted that although Charlie's wife Margaret Ann's name was not on any of his Sun compositions, she played an indivisible part not just in his life but in his music. They were high school sweethearts who shared a subscription to *Down Beat* in a town that had no other subscribers, and as his career progressed, she went on to write some of his most emotionally direct and personal songs. Try "Life's Little Ups and Downs" for a start.

WHAT'D I SAY

Jerry Lee Lewis and His Pumping Piano

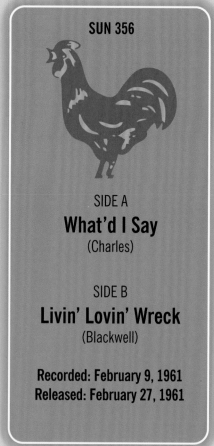

Recorded in Nashville on February 9, 1961, two days before "Who Will the Next Fool Be," and released on the same day, "What'd I Say" represented the resurrection of Jerry Lee for a minute or two prior to his resurfacing as a number-one country artist in the late '60s and early '70s. After a period of time during which he was preoccupied by other business (including radio, his first love, and, improbably enough, an Arkansas zinc mine), it was no accident that Sam should be drawn back into the studio by two artists who were not just his favorites on the current Sun roster but, unquestionably, two of his favorite artists of all time.

Jerry Lee had been working on "What'd I Say," Ray Charles's big 1959 pop hit (his first), in Memphis for some time, but he had never been able to get it right—too fast, even faster, never the right feel. Here, with the same Nashville "A-team" line-up that would accompany Charlie Rich, he took a more measured approach—the raw, almost out-of-control vocals of the Memphis sessions were replaced by a calm air of bacchanalian assurance, and the record was more compact in sound as well as spirit. But most of all it was Jerry's playing that set the tone and, with no other instrument competing for the lead, Jerry Lee offers a master class in controlled, *con brio* pianistics. The record in fact is marred only by a cooing chorus, no match for Ray Charles's unrestrained Raelettes. But surely we can overlook that for the sheer hubris of Jerry Lee's challenge and the spontaneous triumph of the moment. (It's worth noting that Jerry Lee Lewis would soon embark on a thirty-day tour with Jackie Wilson, in which these two extravagantly gifted performers would go head-to-head every night in a succession of Black clubs in what was billed without exaggeration as "The Battle of the Century.")

SUN 356

SIDE A
What'd I Say
(Charles)

SIDE B
Livin' Lovin' Wreck
(Blackwell)

Recorded: February 9, 1961
Released: February 27, 1961

Right: Guitarist Roland Janes watches Jerry Lee Lewis launch off the piano and into legend.

Phillips International 3578

SIDE A
Crawlback
(Frost)

SIDE B
Jelly Roll King
(Frost)

Recorded: April 10, 1962
Released: June 1962

*Left: Frank Frost's only LP on
Phillips International.*

JELLY ROLL KING
Frank Frost and
the Night Hawks

Here we have another welcome return to form by Sam, in 1962; twelve years after his first blues sessions, Sam embraced its "gutbucket" expression once again in his new space-age-designed Sam C. Phillips Recording Studio in Memphis. Frank Frost in person was as off-kilter as any of the older bluesmen that Sam had recorded, and his two bandmates, henceforth to be called the Jelly Roll Kings, were just as individualistic, with drummer Sam Carr in particular providing a vivid display of rhythmic imperfection. "Jelly Roll King" was, in essence, an evocation of Jimmy Reed's drawling delivery (Frost, like Reed, played guitar and rack harmonica), with a story line about a friend named Cobra Joe that was no more linear than some of Joe Hill Louis's compositions.

The Jelly Roll Kings continued to play, in one form or another, for much of the next thirty-five years, with guitarist Jack Johnson, known as "The Oil Man" because he drove a truck for Shell, establishing a career of his own in the '90s blues revival, and Sam Carr, who used a "minimalist" three-piece kit, playing with any number of prominent bluesmen, including Sonny Boy Williamson and Buddy Guy, over the years. (Check him out in Martin Scorsese's *Feel Like Going Home* blues documentary.) But to Sam none of that mattered. For Sam this session was like going home, and he took great pride in the result. "I was homesick for the blues," he said, and saw "a place in the market for Frank Frost." Maybe so. More to the point, he confessed, "I made the mistake of turning on the mike. I knew I was going to get a fatal disease right there. . . . I just had to record him."

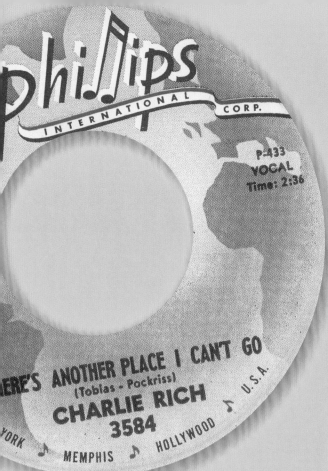

THERE'S ANOTHER PLACE I CAN'T GO
Charlie Rich

Phillips International 3584

SIDE A

There's Another Place I Can't Go
(Tobias—Pockriss)

SIDE B

I Need Your Love
(Rich)

Recorded: August 9, 1962
Released: 1963

Left: Charlie Rich, in the bright-and-melancholy mood.

From a second Charlie Rich Nashville session, once again with some of Nashville's top studio musicians, and once again bringing out close to the best in Charlie. Another song from the same session, "Sittin' and Thinkin'," written in an uncharacteristically straightforward country style, recounts the tale of his own alcoholism. "I hate that song," his wife, Margaret Ann, said whenever he performed it. "You know, it really hits home. That's the real Charlie sure as life."

But it's "There's Another Place I Can't Go," with its bright-and-melancholy, blues-and-jazz-inflected mood, that for me hits home even more. I mean, musically. Its finger-popping beginning, the way that Charlie crisply bites off the lyrics against an occasionally lagging beat, the unlikely part that organ-and-drums play, in fact the whole arrangement—Sam must have gotten a huge kick out of the way it could mix all these unlikely elements and still come together. Charlie was one of the few artists, maybe the only one of his artists, that Sam would go out to see in person, returning night after night to the Sharecropper to listen to him perform. Charlie was almost always drinking heavily, Sam said (Sam was, too), "and yet there was an assurance in Charlie that his music would not desert him. I think the only thing that kept him a little bit out of balance was, how can I do these things that I love to do and still stay commercial enough to work?" Which so often was the problem in the studio. But here he solves it. Or, at least he captures some of Charlie's underlying insouciance, much as he captured his pain with "Who Will the Next Fool Be." It was unquestionably different from that "lost" feeling you got at the club, but as with all the artists Sam recorded in so many different genres, from Howlin' Wolf on, and much in the way that his "slapback" echo effect was intended to conjure up an atmosphere that couldn't be narrowly defined, here, too, he sought to convey a "natural" feel that resided as much in the imagination as in the grooves by inescapably artificial means.

CADILLAC MAN
The Jesters

"Cadillac Man" was one of Sun's final releases—certainly the last in the true, anarchic spirit of Sun. Jim Dickinson, the legendary Memphis iconoclast who sang and played piano on the session, always liked to boast that it was Sam Phillips who produced his recording debut—and maybe it should have been. But it was actually Sam's son Knox who ran the session, while Sam's younger son, Jerry, an individualist in his own right (at twelve and thirteen, he wrestled in small towns all over Arkansas masquerading as The World's Most Perfectly Formed Midget Wrestler against adults who represented the real thing—it's a long story), played rhythm guitar in the band. The song itself was a direct Chuck Berry car-song take-off (think "Maybellene" or "You Can't Catch Me"), put across with a good deal of panache by all involved. And, following in his father's footsteps, Knox fed the drums mike into the piano, creating a distinctively "weird" ("weird-good," as Sam might say) sound.

Sam was impressed when he heard it. And he put it out in February of 1966. But his heart was no longer in it—in just three years he would sell the company (*see p. 219*), and the record would stand as a last, lonely testament of the Sun sound. And when he paid tribute to Jim Dickinson's iconoclastic spirit on the occasion of Dickinson's fiftieth birthday some twenty-five years later, he singled out an obstinate quality that might have stood in for his own. "You know, I never believed that Jim Dickinson was ever ashamed of some of the horrible music he played," Sam joked (I think!), "and that's not easy to do." It was better to dare than to hold back, he emphasized. There was just too damn much precision, not to mention conformity, in the world nowadays. Or, he might well have said, and probably did on many other such occasions, anydays.

SUN 400

SIDE A
My Babe
(Dixon))

SIDE B
Cadillac Man
(Minga)

Recorded: January 22, 1966
Released: February 1966

Right: The Jesters with Sam Phillips. From left: Jerry Phillips, Sam Phillips, Eddie Robertson, Billy Wulfers, Teddy Paige.

ONE MINUTE PAST ETERNITY
Jerry Lee Lewis

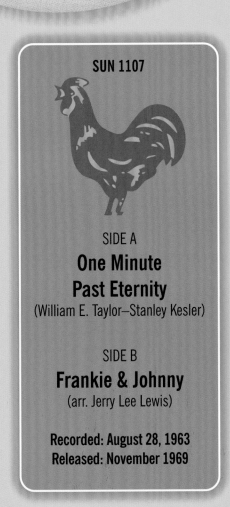

SUN 1107

SIDE A
One Minute Past Eternity
(William E. Taylor–Stanley Kesler)

SIDE B
Frankie & Johnny
(arr. Jerry Lee Lewis)

Recorded: August 28, 1963
Released: November 1969

Left: An unusual studio portrait of Jerry Lee for Sun.

And here once again we catch the future *in situ*. Sam cut this on August 28, 1963, at Jerry Lee Lewis's last recording session for Sun. In so many ways, it was completely out of character—for Sam and Jerry—with a live string section and in-studio chorus contributing their unlikely parts to an unapologetically sentimental country number with a pop twist (cowritten by Stan Kesler). It was not released for another six years, four months after former Mercury/Smash label head Shelby Singleton (it was Shelby who had signed Jerry Lee to Mercury immediately following his last Sun session) had bought Sun Records from Sam. Jerry Lee had at this point had seven straight Top 10 country hits on Smash. Three had hit number 1, and Shelby had already released another track from the same Sun session, "Invitation to Your Party," that went to number 6 almost immediately after the sale. Shelby, whose new independent venture was called SSS [for Shelby S. Singleton] International, was a flamboyant pitchman of the old school, and the new one, too—he is, in fact, the only major-label head of his era not to be elected to the Country Music Hall of Fame, mainly because unlike most of the others he made no attempt to hide his true nature, good or bad. Which may have been the principal trait that led Sam to sell him the label.

There is no question that Shelby bought Sun for its back catalogue. "Sam had no record-club deals," he observed. "He had no foreign deals. And with what I knew about the foreign markets, I knew I could put these records out all over the world and get my money back from foreign releases if I had to." But he saw from the start the potential for contemporary sales, too.

"One Minute Past Eternity," like the rest of the session, was meticulously produced in Sam's most calculatedly relaxed manner. ("Let's try it just almost lazy one time, you know," he says at one point during the session. "Just sing easy and get with it."). It went to number 2 on the country charts, remaining there for sixteen weeks, which was as long as all but one of the Smash hits. And in the aftermath of its success, Shelby released yet another song from the same session, "I Can't Seem to Say Goodbye," and *it* went to number 7. Offering us one more tribute to the talent, vision, and perspicacity of both Sam C. Phillips and Jerry Lee Lewis, and the enduring legacy of Sun.

"Hell, if you're not having fun, it isn't worth doing."

—Sam Phillips

THE HISTORY OF SUN RECORDS,
PART II: BY COLIN ESCOTT

1969-2022

PROLOGUE, PART II:
THE ARRIVAL OF SHELBY SINGLETON

In the era of giddy expansion after World War II, the record business attracted maverick businessmen (and, yes, they were very preponderantly men) who were drawn to the music, or the late hours, or the possibility of unimaginable riches from just one song, or the latitude to act without too much corporate governance. Shelby Singleton found that he was better suited to music than his job at munitions manufacturer Remington Rand. "You have to wait for someone to die," he explained to journalist Jack Hurst. "I went where there was less money and more opportunity."

Above: Shelby (standing, in the dark suit) in the wings at the Grand Ole Opry.

Left: Shelby Singleton touting "The Hit Label," Mercury Records.

Previous spread: Shelby Singleton's creation, the Elvis soundalike, Orion.

Born in Waskom, Texas, in 1931, Singleton married Margaret Ebey and supported her budding music career as Margie Singleton. In 1957, he landed her a deal with Starday Records, and in October that year secured himself a job as Starday's southeastern promotion rep, based in Shreveport, Louisiana. Starday had entered into a brief joint venture with Mercury Records, and when the two companies separated, Singleton remained with Mercury. In February 1961, he was appointed vice president of A&R (artists & repertoire) and sent to Nashville, where he created a presence for Mercury in country music. Several months later he took over some of Mercury's New York A&R duties too.

Today, record producers are usually skilled musicians. Singleton almost proudly knew nothing about music, but had an ear for songs and artists. He rolled tape until he heard something he could sell. He brought country session musicians to New York and R&B singers to Nashville, trying to find the intersection where the sales were. He was involved in hits by George Jones, Clyde McPhatter, Roger Miller, Leroy Van Dyke, and many more. He signed Jerry Lee Lewis away from Sun, too.

"My attorney in New York told me if I went into business for myself and did ten percent of what I did for Mercury I'd make a lot of money," Singleton told journalist Walt Trott. In an earlier account, he'd said his private clairvoyant told him it was time to leave. In January 1967, he tested the waters as an independent producer, scoring with the Hombres' "Let It All Hang Out" on MGM Records. After promoting the record himself, he decided he'd be better off owning a label too. With $1,000, he started SSS Records. The first releases were R&B. In May 1968, he started a country label, Plantation. Moving his company to Belmont Boulevard in Nashville—three miles from the city's Music Row—seemed to imply that Singleton would not be part of the clubby country music establishment. In July, though, he produced the top-selling country record of the year, "Harper Valley P.T.A."

Shelby and staff in front of their new offices at 3106 Belmont Boulevard, Nashville.

"Sam had no record-club deals. He had no foreign deals. And with what I knew about the foreign markets, I knew I could put these records out all over the world. Plus I figured that Johnny Cash was going to get hot."

—Shelby Singleton

HARPER VALLEY P.T.A.

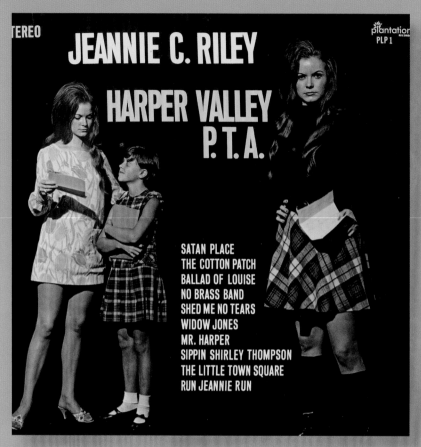

STEREO

plantation RECORDS
PLP 1

JEANNIE C. RILEY

HARPER VALLEY P.T.A.

SATAN PLACE
THE COTTON PATCH
BALLAD OF LOUISE
NO BRASS BAND
SHED ME NO TEARS
WIDOW JONES
MR. HARPER
SIPPIN SHIRLEY THOMPSON
THE LITTLE TOWN SQUARE
RUN JEANNIE RUN

Far Right: Jeannie C. Riley chatting with Shelby Singleton at the console. Jerry Kennedy stands at top.

The hit song "Harper Valley P.T.A." wasn't on Sun, but it played a crucial role in the label's story.

When radio station WENO in Madison, Tennessee, held its listener appreciation day in 1967, the program director, Paul Perry, called in favors to lay on entertainment. Songwriter Tom T. Hall, newly signed to Mercury Records as an artist, was there. So were Leon Ashley and his wife, Margie Singleton—singers and co-owners of Ashley Records in nearby Hendersonville. (Margie was the ex-wife of future Sun Records owner, Shelby Singleton). As food was served to the entertainers, Singleton asked Hall to write a song for her along the lines of "Ode to Billie Joe." Driving south of Nashville, Hall saw a sign for the Harpeth Valley Utility District, and it triggered a memory of a woman in his home-town who had taken on P.T.A. members for their indiscretions. "I wrote ["Harper Valley P.T.A."] sitting at my red checkered tablecloth," he wrote later. "I don't recall that it took more than an hour or so, but I had the idea for twenty years." The copyright notice was filed on December 26, 1967.

When Hall took the song to Leon Ashley and Margie Singleton, Singleton was on tour. Ashley handed it to one of their artists, Alice Joy, whose husband worked for WENO. Joy's recording was never released, but Hall's publisher gave a dub to Shelby Singleton. It sat in a desk for six months before WENO's Paul Perry drew Singleton's attention to Jeannie C. Riley, then working as a receptionist while moonlighting as a demo singer. Singleton heard the feistiness that would bring "Harper Valley P.T.A." to life, so he booked a session.

Seven months after the song was copyrighted, the artist, song lead sheets, producer, songwriter, musicians, and arranger were all in the studio. It was the evening of July 26, 1968, shortly after

"The day my mama socked it to the Harper Valley P.T.A." —Jeannie C. Riley

Riley got off work. The arranger and leader was Jerry Kennedy, who played fretted Dobro. Kennedy had taken over Singleton's role as the head of Mercury Records' country music division, and had just signed Tom T. Hall. It was a tight-knit world. Hall had been at a bar on Nashville's Broadway when he heard about the session, so he drove over. Singleton's second wife, Barbara, asked him if she (Barbara) could change the original concluding words from "The day mama broke up the Harper Valley P.T.A." to "The day my mama socked it to the Harper Valley P.T.A." Riley strutted through the lyrics, with Kennedy sustaining and building the tension between lines. The session was over by 9 p.m., but the musicians hung around to hear the song again. "There was a loud roar" from the musicians after it played, Hall remembered. Typically, he "picked up a beer and melted into the night." Singleton tested his hunch that he was onto something by taking an acetate to WSM's all-night deejay Ralph Emery. Call-in lines lit up.

That weekend, Singleton serviced "Harper Valley P.T.A." by air express to every major country station. Kennedy had spent the weekend in Gatlinburg, Tennessee, and by the time he drove home on Monday, he was hearing "Harper Valley P.T.A.." on the radio. It entered the country and pop charts on August 24, 1968, reaching the top of both. Hall wrote many songs, but none bigger; Riley never had another epic hit, and neither did Singleton. Sales figures are elusive, but between singles, LPs, cassettes, and eight-tracks, it was, as those in the business liked to say, tonnage. Facing the prospect of a hefty tax bill, Singleton decided to acquire some assets. He'd contacted Sam Phillips on behalf of Mercury Records in 1962, essentially suggesting that Sun would become one of Mercury's production affiliates, but the talk had fizzled out. This time, Phillips was listening.

1969

SELLING SUN

Above: July 1969: Sam Phillips (left) sells Sun Records to Shelby Singleton (center) while Singleton's New York attorney, Stuart Silfen (standing), and Singleton's executive vice president Nobel Bell look on.

In the wake of "Harper Valley P.T.A.," Shelby Singleton expanded fast.

He built a studio, bought labels (including Sun and New York's Red Bird Records), and publishing companies. He looked and played the part of a record mogul. When Jack Hurst interviewed him in 1969, he found "a blocky man with theatrical sideburns and an ashtray of black cigarillo butts." In an interview with *Billboard* magazine the following year, Singleton said, "I have to keep moving or all the challenge is gone."

Back in 1962, when Singleton was vice president of Mercury Records, he approached Sam Phillips about taking over Sun's past and future output. The talk even reached the trade papers, but nothing was consummated. They picked up the discussion in late 1968. By then Singleton was heading his own company and was flush with cash from "Harper Valley P.T.A." Phillips and Singleton reached an agreement in June 1969. Phillips was predisposed to work

with Singleton. He'd
always liked him and admired his acumen
and hustle. Phillips would get $1 million, but the clincher was probably
Singleton's assurance that Sun would not end up as a minor asset of a vast corporation. As
additional enticements, Phillips would get 20 percent of a newly incorporated entity, Sun International Corporation, and would retain the music publishing. Publishing was passive income.
Mailbox money, they used to say. Until the copyrights came up for renewal, Phillips published
nearly all the songs that Johnny Cash and Carl Perkins recorded at Sun, and some songs that
Jerry Lee Lewis recorded. The rate, 2¢ per song per copy sold (customarily split with the songwriter), hadn't changed since 1909, but could still add up.

Singleton sent a truck to Memphis to get the tapes. He was in a hurry. Cash had rarely been
absent from the upper or lower reaches of the country chart since 1955. In 1969, he was not
only one of the biggest country stars but was also selling to kids who wouldn't otherwise go
near country music. His live recording of "Folsom Prison Blues" (*see p. 141*) at the prison
itself went to the top of the country chart in 1968, followed by his recording of Carl Perkins's
"Daddy Sang Bass." Perkins was touring with Cash, making him as visible as he'd been since
1956. And then on June 7, 1969, the first episode of *The Johnny Cash Show* aired on ABC. On
July 1, Singleton and Phillips made their new deal official, and one week later Cash's "A Boy
Named Sue" began its ascent to the top of the country chart and number two on the pop chart.
By August, Singleton had two volumes of Cash's hits on the racks. Both, he said, sold more
than 180,000 copies. Three more Cash LPs on Sun were out by year-end, and the good news
for Singleton didn't end there.

Back in 1963, Singleton had signed Jerry Lee Lewis to Mercury Records. Two records darted
in and out of the Billboard Hot 100, neither getting any higher than ninety-one, but then in 1968,
Lewis reinvented himself as a country singer. As Phillips and Singleton were beginning their
business talks, "To Make Love Sweeter for You" was closing in on the top of the country chart.

This page: Cashing in.

*Opposite: Shelby showing off his successes on
the Hot 100 and Hot Country Singles charts.*

STEREO

SUN-114

Jerry Lee Lewis
a taste of country

I CAN'T SEEM TO SAY GOODBYE
I LOVE YOU SO MUCH IT HURTS
I'M THROWING RICE
GOODNIGHT IRENE
YOUR CHEATIN' HEART
AM I TO BE THE ONE
CRAZY ARMS
NIGHT TRAIN TO MEMPHIS
AS LONG AS I LIVE
YOU WIN AGAIN
IT HURT ME SO

"I have to keep moving or all the challenge is gone."

—Shelby Singleton

Left: By 1969, Jerry Lee Lewis was a country star.

Lewis's wife, Myra Gale, was now twenty-four and they'd had two kids. Plenty of other scandals had overtaken that one. To Singleton's surprise, he found unissued songs from Lewis's last Sun sessions that were essentially a blueprint for country stardom, and lost no time issuing them. During the week that men first walked on the moon, Singleton published a full-page advertisement in *Billboard* in the form of a fake newspaper. The banner headline in relatively small type was "Astronauts Walk on Moon." Beneath that, in bigger type, was "Jerry Lee Lewis Hits on Sun." Both would have seemed equally unlikely not so long before. And then, in 1973, Charlie Rich became a top-selling country artist, giving Singleton the opening to dust off Rich's earlier work.

The one Sun artist Singleton did *not* have was Elvis Presley, and he tried to make good on that by signing an impersonator, Jimmy Ellis, whom he reinvented as "Orion." Wearing a bejeweled mask, Orion invited Elvis's legions of fans to believe that Elvis had not died but had returned to Sun.

As Singleton's domestic releases dried up, his overseas licensees began exploring the deep catalogue, including the blues recordings that had gone almost untouched for twenty or thirty years. There lay Shelby Singleton's enduring contribution to Sun's legacy. He allowed his licensees uncounted and unbilled hours in his studio listening to tapes and making compilations. At one point, Columbia Records had tried to buy the Sun catalogue from Phillips in an attempt to get Cash's old recordings off the market. Had they done so, Sun Records as a brand would have disappeared and the tapes would have been consigned to a corporate tape vault, largely inaccessible. On Singleton's watch, Phillips's achievement was writ large——on the Sun label.

Above: If you don't have an Elvis, make one: Jimmy Ellis as the masked Orion.

Right top: Orion's 1978 debut album showing him rising from (what some thought was) Elvis's coffin. It was quickly pulled off the shelves and resleeved (bottom).

THE SUN COMPILATIONS

When Shelby Singleton bought Sun in 1969, Sam Phillips's astonishing ear for talent was still fabled within the business, but few saw that his work would be canonized as one of the cornerstones of modern popular music. Phillips might have been one of those few.

As early as 1961, Phillips issued a compilation, *Sun's Gold Hits*, optimistically subtitled "Volume 1." Back then, very few hits compilations were titled after the record label, but Phillips already understood that the Sun brand itself had cachet. Three years later he issued a Johnny Cash compilation, *Original Sun Sound of Johnny Cash*. Phillips's flow of albums stopped there, but in 1966 his British licensee, London Records, made the first deep dive into the catalogue with *The Blues Came Down from Memphis*—an anthology of Phillips's blues recordings with six mouthwateringly rare Sun labels on the front jacket. Few even knew then that Sun had started with blues.

After the sale, Shelby Singleton opened the vault in a way that Phillips never did. There would be Sun compilations at every price point, from box sets costing hundreds of dollars to 99¢ truck-stop cassettes. Concurrently, rock music journalism took root. Until then, journalists hadn't scratched far beneath the surface of popular music. What's Ringo's pet peeve? That kind of thing. There had been a few long-form articles in general interest magazines, but it wasn't until the advent of *Rolling Stone* in 1967 and *Creem* two years later that writing about rock music's past and present rose to the level of classics and jazz. That brought Phillips's achievement into sharper focus.

In Europe, Singleton licensed Sun to Philips Records. Based in the Netherlands, Philips owned Singleton's former employer, Mercury Records, and bought rights to the name *Phillips International* from Sam Phillips. The first Sun rockabilly compilation appeared on Philips in 1973. In 1975, the European rights passed to Charly Records. Soon after that, Singleton revealed

Left: Sam Phillips' first compilation album, Sun's Gold Hits, *1961.*

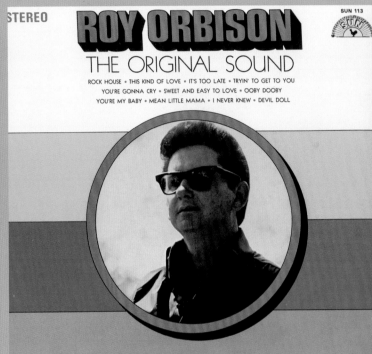

This page and next: The last album issued on Sun under Phillips' ownership was *The Original Sun Sound of Johnny Cash*. It's followed on this page and the next with some of the compilation albums issued during Shelby Singleton's ownership.

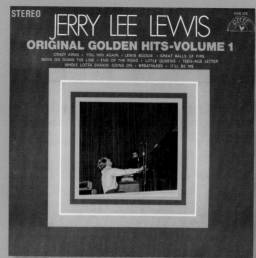

the existence of 1,260 boxes of session tapes in his basement. In those outtake boxes lay the full story of Sun Records.

From the dawn of the LP in 1948, jazz labels had been issuing outtakes and rejected tunes. Jazz outtakes often yielded vividly different solos or arrangements, but Sun's outtake reels were revealing in other ways. Phillips can sometimes be heard chastising and encouraging his artists. On a 1958 reel, he engaged Jerry Lee Lewis in a fiery discussion about religion and rock 'n' roll. Phillips's original goal was to be an attorney, and his trial lawyer-like persuasiveness comes through, but it's no match for Lewis's fanaticism. Phillips tries to tell Lewis that he can play rock 'n' roll yet still do good. Lewis is having none of it. *"How can the Devil save souls?"* he yells. "What are you *talking about*? Man I got *the Devil* in me! If I didn't have, I'd be a Christian!" On another reel we hear Johnny Cash chiding his plaintive but technically inadequate guitarist, Luther Perkins. "What're you *doing*, Luther? What're you doing? Key of A, please." Hidden away on other reels were artists never even known to have recorded for Sun.

Such a wealth of material could only be covered in box sets, and they came soon enough. Charly Records began with a modest three-LP box set, *The Sun Story*, in 1980. Ever more ambitious sets followed on Charly, Bear Family, Rhino, and other labels. Reverting to Phillips's original love of the single, Bear Family issued six box sets of every Sun, Flip, and Phillips International single. Phillips offered his approval.

> ## "How can the Devil save souls? What are you talking about? Man I got the Devil in me!"
>
> —Jerry Lee Lweis

EPILOGUE

Left: The original Memphis Recording Service, where it all began, today.

In 1968, a few months before the discussions between Shelby Singleton and Sam Phillips began their tortuous path, Shelby brought in his brother, John, initially to manage his music publishing division and, a few years later, to become his equal partner. Eventually John took over management of the entire company, more so as Shelby's health began to fail in the early 2000s. John became president of Sun in 2000.

Shelby Singleton died in 2009, six years after Sam Phillips, and Sun Entertainment Corporation continued to thrive. In 2020, the Singleton brothers' entire holdings were purchased by Primary Wave Music, a company that specializes in working with legendary songwriters, artists, and music brands. Primary Wave is currently restoring the original master tapes and cataloguing the memorabilia and unreleased recordings for future projects. Additional plans include an expansion of the merchandise line, a docuseries, scripted series, and podcast, as well as the expansion of the Sun Diner. The company's goal is to carry forward the legacy of Sun Records, ensuring that it will always be recognized as the birthplace of rock and roll.

Sam Phillips started Sun Records out of frustration, but with a clear conviction that he was in the right place at the right time. His belief that Memphis was the crossroads of American music grew almost messianic. He had an artistic compass in the same way that some record producers have a commercial compass, but he couldn't ignore the commercial here and now. When he designed his first piece of stationery, he coined a slogan: "Consistently better records for higher profits." It was an endearingly modest boast at the time, but those consistently better records are still the beating heart of popular music. So much old music is sucked into the void with those who once listened to it. You had to be there. Recordings that span the years are those in which the singer, the song, and the listener become one. Everything extraneous is stripped away. The producer's job is to create the conditions in which that can happen. Fight down every urge to make it more complex than it needs to be. And to not be afraid of something that wasn't there before.

That's what Sam Phillips did. That's why we're still listening.

As a tireless and enthusiastic ambassador not only for his father's work but for Memphis music, Knox Phillips (1945-2020) connected the Memphis spirit, his father's legacy, and his own love of the music to the world stage. As a record producer and engineer at Sam Phillips Recording Service, he worked on albums by some of music's greatest stars, including Willie Nelson, Jerry Lee Lewis, Jerry Jeff Walker, John Prine, and The Amazing Rhythm Aces. He also supported struggling artists by giving them free studio time and was instrumental in establishing the Memphis chapter of the National Academy of Recording Arts and Sciences in 1973. Knox Phillips was inducted into The Memphis Music Hall of Fame in 2013.

AFTERWORD

Left: Sam Phillips (center) with his sons Knox (left) and Jerry (right).

I'll never forget the night my father, Sam Phillips, brought home Elvis's first record. It was a 45 RPM pressing of "That's All Right" and "Blue Moon of Kentucky," and he was so excited he wanted my mother Becky, my younger brother Jerry, and me to hear it right away. I don't remember if he'd played us the acetate first, but the sight of that little yellow label going round and round on our vinyl-covered black-and-white High Fidelity record changer, the sound that was generated by that Sun 45, and the sheer excitement on my father's face, as if this was the summation of everything he had been working toward for so long, as if this was the differentness that he had been preaching—I can't divide it, it's all encapsulated in that one moment. Then everything changed.

Now the world knows my father for the music he gave us. If he were here, he'd probably tell you about differentness, passionate conviction, inspiring people to be themselves no matter what that self might be, and loving extreme self-expression. Sam knew music had the timeless characteristic of capturing the "heart . . . and the soul." Music producers can't quantify that, but great producers can recognize it when they hear it. Listen to any Sun record and you will hear an expression of belief in freedom and individuality; the music embodies a sense of human potential and spirit that was Sun Records and all the music that Sam Phillips recorded.

The world also knows Sam Phillips as a great man, and a great revolutionary, and I do, too. But I feel like, growing up, my brother Jerry and I—and all of Sam's artists from B. B. King, Howlin' Wolf, Little Milton, The Prisonaires, Roscoe Gordon, Ike Turner, Jackie Brenston, and Rufus Thomas to Elvis Presley, Carl Perkins, Johnny Cash, Jerry Lee Lewis, Roy Orbison, Billy Lee Riley, Sonny Burgess, Bill Justis, Charlie Rich, and so many others—we all saw a side of him that the public didn't necessarily see. Because Sam Phillips was a great teacher, too.

My father felt like he had a mission in life—not to teach from a lesson plan or written-out text, but to teach *everyone* with whom he came in contact how to be the best individual human being that they could possibly be. In other words, if you were going to be a musician, be the best musician, *in your own way*, that you could be, taking into account your individual strengths and weaknesses, never measuring yourself against someone else, but only against the ideal of expressing yourself. If you were a yardman, or a professional wrestler, be the best yardman or professional wrestler you could be. Trust yourself. That was his lesson. That was *everything* for Sam. Be yourself—and if other people didn't like it, well, c'est la vie.

I have always thought that my father was the walking definition of the independent entrepreneur—a daring leader, unconventional in his approach to everything from art to business, who had a total belief and confidence in himself, and a sharing, giving, charitable spirit. In general, people don't realize that the reason they have reacted so strongly, so deeply over the years to those wonderful Sun records—and all of Sam's work—was because they were feeling Sam's presence in those recordings. He loved every moment he spent with every artist, family member, friend, and fan and left a piece of himself with each and every one of us. Those memories will always be instructive, and he will be forever present.

—Knox Phillips, 2001

THE COMPLETE SUN DISCOGRAPHY

Editor's Note: Creating a definitive list such as this is often tricky, as the label information tended to change depending on where the record was being pressed. The artist names and song titles presented here reflect the way they appeared on the initial pressing. Record-keeping of release dates at Sun was not a perfect science, either; the release dates listed here are based on the best research available. Finally, as there were no A and B sides noted on these singles, for consistency the songs for each record are listed in order of their master recording (or "U") number indicated on the label.

Sun Records: The Singles

174
Jackie Boy and Little Walter
Blues in My Condition
Sellin' My Whiskey
Not issued

175
Johnny London—Alto Wizard
Drivin' Slow
Flat Tire
April 1952

176
Walter Bradford and the Big City Four
Dreary Nights
Nuthin' but the Blues
April 1952

177
Handy Jackson
Got My Application, Baby
Trouble (Will Bring You Down)
January 1953

178
Joe Hill Louis
We All Gotta Go Sometime
She May Be Yours (But She Comes to See Me Sometime)
January 1953

179
Willie Nix (The Memphis Blues Boy)
Seems Like a Million Years
Baker Shop Boogie
January 1953

180
Jimmy and Walter
Easy
Before Long
March 1953

181
Rufus "Hound Dog" Thomas Jr.
Bear Cat (The Answer to "Hound Dog")
Walkin' in the Rain
March 1953

182
Dusty Brooks and His Tones
Heaven or Fire
Tears and Wine
March 1953

183
D. A. Hunt
Lonesome Ol' Jail
Greyhound Blues
June 1953

184
Big Memphis Marainey—Onzie Horne Combo
Call Me Anything, but Call Me Baby, No, No!
June 1953

185
Jimmy DeBerry
Take a Little Chance
Time Has Made a Change
June 1953

186
The Prisonaires
Baby Please
Just Walkin' in the Rain
July 8, 1953

187
Little Junior's Blue Flames
Feelin' Good
Fussin' and Fightin' Blues
July 8, 1953

188
Rufus Thomas, Jr.
Tiger Man (King of the Jungle)
Save That Money
July 8, 1953

189
The Prisonaires—Confined to Tennessee State Penitentiary, Nashville
My God Is Real
Softly and Tenderly
August 1953

190
Ripley Cotton Choppers
Silver Bells
Blues Waltz
September 1953

191
The Prisonaires—Confined to Tennessee State Penitentiary, Nashville
A Prisoner's Prayer
I Know
November 1, 1953

192
Little Junior's Blue Flames
Love My Baby
Mystery Train
November 1, 1953

193
Doctor Ross
Come Back Baby
Chicago Breakdown
December 24, 1953

194
Little Milton
Beggin' My Baby
Somebody Told Me
December 24, 1953

195
Billy "The Kid" Emerson
No Teasing Around
If Lovin' is Believing
February 20, 1954

196
Hot Shot Love
Wolf Call Boogie
Harmonica Jam
February 20, 1954

197
Earl Peterson—Michigan's Singing Cowboy
Boogie Blues
In the Dark
February 20, 1954

198
Howard Seratt
Troublesome Waters
I Must Be Saved
February 20, 1954

199
James Cotton
My Baby
Straighten Up, Baby
April 15, 1954

200
Little Milton
If You Love Me
Alone and Blue
April 15, 1954

201
Hardrock Gunter
Fallen Angel
Gonna Dance All Night
May 1, 1954

202
Doug Poindexter and the
Starlite Wranglers
Now She Cares No More
My Kind of Carrying On
May 1, 1954

203
Billy "The Kid" Emerson
I'm Not Going Home
The Woodchuck
May 1, 1954

204
Raymond Hill
The Snuggle
Bourbon Street Jump
May 1, 1954

205
Harmonica Frank
The Great Medical Menagerist
Rockin' Chair Daddy
May 1, 1954

206
James Cotton
Cotton Crop Blues
Hold Me in Your Arms
July 1, 1954

207
The Prisonaires
There Is Love in You
What'll You Do Next
July 1, 1954

208
Buddy Cunningham
Why Do I Cry
Right or Wrong
July 15, 1954

209
Elvis Presley with Scotty and Bill
That's All Right
Blue Moon of Kentucky
July 19, 1954

210
Elvis Presley—Scotty and Bill
I Don't Care If the Sun Don't Shine
Good Rockin' Tonight
September 22, 1954

211
Malcolm Yelvington and the Star
Rhythm Boys
Drinkin' Wine Spodee-O-Dee
Just Rolling Along
November 10, 1954

212
Doctor Ross
The Boogie Disease
Juke Box Boogie
November 10, 1954

213
The Jones Brothers
Every Night
Look to Jesus
January 8, 1955

214
Billy "The Kid" Emerson
Move Baby Move
When It Rains It Pours
January 8, 1955

215
Elvis Presley with Scotty and Bill
Milkcow Blues Boogie
You're a Heartbreaker
January 8, 1955

216
Slim Rhodes
Don't Believe (Vocal: Brad Suggs)
Uncertain Love (Vocal: Dusty & Dot)
April 1, 1955

217
Elvis Presley
I'm Left, You're Right, She's Gone
Baby Let's Play House
April 25, 1955

218
Sammy Lewis and the Willie
Johnson Combo
I Feel So Worried
So Long Baby Goodbye
April 25, 1955

219
Billy "The Kid" Emerson
Red Hot
No Greater Love
June 21, 1955

220
Little Milton
Lookin' for My Baby
Homesick for My Baby
June 21, 1955

221
Johnny Cash and the Tennessee Two
Hey, Porter!
Cry! Cry! Cry!
June 21, 1955

222
The Five Tinos
Don't Do That!
Sitting By My Window
June 21, 1955

223
Elvis Presley with Scotty and Bill
Mystery Train
I Forgot to Remember to Forget
August 1, 1955

224
Carl Perkins
Let the Juke Box Keep on Playing
Gone, Gone, Gone
August 1, 1955

225
Slim Rhodes
The House of Sin (Vocal: Dusty & Dot)
*Are You Ashamed of Me (Vocal: Brad
Suggs)*
August 1, 1955

THE COMPLETE SUN DISCOGRAPHY

(Continued)

Sun Records: The Singles (Continued)

226
Eddie Snow
Ain't That Right
Bring Your Love Back Home to Me
August 1, 1955

227
Rosco Gordon
Just Love Me Baby
Weeping Blues
September 1955

228
Smokey Joe
The Signifying Monkey
Listen to Me Baby
September 15, 1955

229
Maggie Sue Wimberly
How Long
Daydreams Come True
December 1955

230
The Miller Sisters
There's No Right Way to Do Me Wrong
You Can Tell Me
January 15, 1956

231
Charlie Feathers
Defrost Your Heart
A Wedding Gown of White
December 1955

232
Johnny Cash and the Tennessee Two
So Doggone Lonesome
Folsom Prison Blues
December 15, 1955

233
Billy "The Kid" Emerson
Little Fine Healthy Thing
Something For Nothing
January 15, 1956

234
Carl Perkins
Blue Suede Shoes
Honey, Don't!
December 1955

235
Carl Perkins
Sure to Fall
Tennessee
Not issued

236
Jimmy Haggett
No More, No More
They Call Our Love a Sin
December 1955

237
Roscoe Gordon
The Chicken (Dance with You)
Love for You Baby
December 1955

238
Slim Rhodes
Gonna Romp and Stomp
Bad Girl
April 1956

239
Warren Smith
Rock 'n' Roll Ruby
I'd Rather Be Safe Than Sorry
April 1956

240
Jack Earls and the Jimbos
Slow Down
A Fool for Lovin' You
April 1956

241
Johnny Cash and the Tennessee Two
Get Rhythm
I Walk the Line
April 1956

242
Roy Orbison and the Teen Kings
Ooby Dooby
Go! Go! Go!
May 1956

243
Carl Perkins
Boppin' the Blues
All Mama's Children
May 1956

244
Jean Chapel
Welcome to the Club
I Won't Be Rockin' Tonight
June 1956

245
Billy Riley
Trouble Bound
Rock with Me Baby
May 1956

246
Malcolm Yelvington
Rockin' with My Baby
It's Me Baby
August 3, 1956

247
Sonny Burgess
Red Headed Woman
We Wanna Boogie
August 3, 1956

248
The Rhythm Rockers
Juke Box Help Me Find My Baby
Fiddle Bop
August 3, 1956

249
Carl Perkins
I'm Sorry I'm Not Sorry
Dixie Fried
August 3, 1956

250
Warren Smith
Black Jack David
Ubangi Stomp
September 24, 1956

251
Orbison and the Teen Kings
You're My Baby
Rockhouse
September 24, 1956

252
Kenneth Parchman
Love Crazy Baby
I Feel Like Rockin'
Not Issued

253
Barbara Pittman
I Need a Man
No Matter Who's to Blame
September 24, 1956

254
Ray Harris
Come On Little Mama
Where'd You Stay Last Night
September 24, 1956

255
The Miller Sisters
Ten Cats Down
Finders Keepers
August 3, 1956

256
Slim Rhodes
Take and Give
Do What I Do
November 21, 1956

257
Rosco Gordon
Shoobie Oobie
Cheese and Crackers
November 21, 1956

258
Johnny Cash and the Tennessee Two
Train of Love
There You Go
November 21, 1956

259
Jerry Lee Lewis with His
Pumping Piano
Crazy Arms
End of the Road
December 1, 1956

260
Billy Riley and His Little Green Men
Flyin' Saucers Rock and Roll
I Want You Baby
January 23, 1957

261
Carl Perkins
Matchbox
Your True Love
January 23, 1957

262
Ernie Chaffin
Feelin' Low
Lonesome for My Baby
January 23, 1957

263
Sonny Burgess
Restless
Ain't Got a Thing
January 24, 1957

264
Glenn Honeycutt
I'll Be Around
I'll Wait Forever
January 24, 1957

265
Roy Orbison and the Roses
Sweet and Easy to Love
Devil Doll
January 24, 1957

266
Johnny Cash and the Tennessee Two
Don't Make Me Go
Next in Line
March 15, 1957

267
Jerry Lee Lewis
Whole Lotta Shakin' Going On
It'll Be Me
March 15, 1957

268
Warren Smith
So Long I'm Gone
Miss Froggie
April 15, 1957

269
Wade and Dick, the College Kids
Bop Bop Baby
Don't Need Your Lovin' Baby
April 15, 1957

270
Jim Williams
Please Don't Cry over Me
That Depends on You
September 14, 1957

271
Rudi Richardson
Fools Hall of Fame
Why Should I Cry
April 15, 1957

272
Ray Harris
Greenback Dollar, Watch and Chain
Foolish Heart
June 1957

273
Mack Self
Easy to Love
Everyday
June 1957

274
Carl Perkins
Forever Yours
That's Right
August 15, 1957

275
Ernie Chaffin
I'm Lonesome
Laughin' and Jokin'
August 15, 1957

276
Edwin Bruce
More Than Yesterday
Rock Boppin' Baby
August 15, 1957

277
Billy Riley and His Little Green Men
Red Hot
Pearly Lee
September 14, 1957

278
Tommy Blake and the Rhythm Rebels
Flat Foot Sam
Lordy Hoody
September 14, 1957

279
Johnny Cash and the Tennessee Two
Home of the Blues
Give My Love to Rose
September 14, 1957

280
Dickey Lee and the Collegiates
Memories Never Grow Old
Good Lovin'
October 12, 1957

281
Jerry Lee Lewis and His
Pumping Piano
Great Balls of Fire
You Win Again
November 3, 1957

Sun Records: The Singles (Continued)

282
Dick Penner
Your Honey Love
Cindy Lou
November 3, 1957

283
Johnny Cash and the Tennessee Two
Ballad of a Teenage Queen
Big River
December 1957

284
Roy Orbison
Chicken Hearted
I Like Love
December 1957

285
Sonny Burgess
My Bucket's Got a Hole in It
Sweet Misery
December 1957

286
Warren Smith
I've Got Love If You Want It
I Fell in Love
December 1957

287
Carl Perkins—The Rockin'
Guitar Man
Glad All Over
Lend Me Your Comb
December 1957

288
Jerry Lee Lewis and His
Pumping Piano
Down the Line
Breathless
February 1958

289
Billy Riley and His Little Green Men
Wouldn't You Know
Baby Please Don't Go
February 1958

290
Rudy Grayzell
I Think of You
Judy
April 9, 1958

291
Jack Clement
Ten Years
Your Lover Boy
April 9, 1958

292
Edwin Bruce
Sweet Woman
Part of My Life
April 9, 1958

293
The Sunrays
Love Is a Stranger
The Lonely Hours
April 9, 1958

294
Magel Priesman
I Feel So Blue
Memories of You
April 9, 1958

295
Johnny Cash and the Tennessee Two
Guess Things Happen That Way
Come in Stranger
April 9, 1958

296
Jerry Lee Lewis and His
Pumping Piano
High School Confidential
Fools Like Me
April 9, 1958

297
Dickey Lee and the Collegiates
Fool, Fool, Fool
Dreamy Nights
April 9, 1958

298
Ray Smith
So Young
Right Behind You Baby
April 9, 1958

299
Gene Simmons
Drinkin' Wine
I Done Told You
April 9, 1958

300
Tommy Blake
Sweetie Pie
I Dig You Baby
June 1958

301
Jerry Lee Lewis and His
Pumping Piano
The Return of Jerry Lee
(Narration by George and Louis)
Lewis Boogie
June 1958

302
Johnny Cash and the Tennessee Two
The Ways of a Woman in Love
You're the Nearest Thing to Heaven
May 1958

303
Jerry Lee Lewis and His
Pumping Piano
Break-Up
I'll Make It All Up to You
August 10, 1958

304
Sonny Burgess
Thunderbird
Itchy
August 10, 1958

305
Rosco Gordon
Sally Jo
Torro
September 20, 1958

306
Jimmy Isle
I've Been Waitin'
Diamond Ring
October 25, 1958

307
Ernie Chaffin
(Nothing Can Change) My Love
for You
Born to Lose
October 15, 1958

308
Ray Smith
Why, Why, Why
You Made a Hit
October 25, 1958

309
Johnny Cash and the Tennessee Two
I Just Thought You'd Like to Know
It's Just About Time
November 12, 1958

310
Vernon Taylor
Breeze
Today Is a Blue Day
November 12, 1958

311
Jack Clement
The Black Haired Man
Wrong
November 20, 1958

312
Jerry Lee Lewis and His
Pumping Piano
It Hurt Me So
I'll Sail My Ship Alone
November 20, 1958

313
Billy Riley
Down by the Riverside
No Name Girl
February 1, 1959

314
Warren Smith
Sweet, Sweet Girl
Goodbye Mr. Love
February 15, 1959

315
Onie Wheeler
Jump Right Out of This Jukebox
Tell 'Em Off
February 15, 1959

316
Johnny Cash and the Tennessee Two
Thanks a Lot
Luther Played the Boogie
February 15, 1959

317
Jerry Lee Lewis and His
Pumping Piano
Lovin' Up a Storm
Big Blon' Baby
February 15, 1959

318
Jimmy Isle
Time Will Tell
Without a Love
March 23, 1959

319
Ray Smith
Rockin' Bandit
Sail Away
March 23, 1959

320
Ernie Chaffin
Don't Ever Leave
Miracle of You
April 27, 1959

321
Johnny Cash and the Tennessee Two
I Forgot to Remember to Forget
Katy Too
June 2, 1959

322
Bill Riley
One More Time
Got the Water Boiling Baby
June 2, 1959

323
Alton and Jimmy
Have Faith in My Love
No More Crying the Blues
June 2, 1959

324
Jerry Lee Lewis and His
Pumping Piano
Let's Talk About Us
The Ballad of Billy Joe
June 15, 1959

325
Vernon Taylor
Sweet and Easy to Love
Mystery Train
July 16, 1959

326
Jerry McGill and the Topcoats
I Wanna Make Sweet Love
Lovestruck
August 11, 1959

327
Johnny Powers
With Your Love, with Your Kiss
Be Mine, All Mine
September 15, 1959

328
Sherry Crane
Willie, Willie
Winnie the Parakeet
August 11, 1959

329
Will Mercer
You're Just My Kind
Ballad of St. Marks
September 15, 1959

330
Jerry Lee Lewis and His
Pumping Piano
Little Queenie
I Could Never Be Ashamed of You
September 15, 1959

331
Johnny Cash and the Tennessee Two
You Tell Me
Goodbye Little Darlin'
September 15, 1959

332
Jimmy Isle
What a Life
Together
September 15, 1959

333
Ray B. Anthony
Alice Blue Gown
St. Louis Blues
October 25, 1959

334
Johnny Cash and the Tennessee Two
Straight A's in Love
I Love You Because
December 31, 1959

335
Tracy Pendarvis and the Swampers
A Thousand Guitars
Is It Too Late?
January 1960

336
Mack Owen
Walkin' and Talkin'
Somebody Like You
January 1960

337
Jerry Lee Lewis with tThe Gene
Lowery Singers
Old Black Joe
Baby Baby Bye Bye
March 1960

Sun Records: The Singles (Continued)

338
Paul Richy with the Gene
Lowery Singers
The Legend of the Big Steeple
Broken Hearted Willie
March 8, 1960

339
Rayburn Anthony
Who's Gonna Shoe Your Pretty
Little Feet
(with the Gene Lowery Singers)
There's No Tomorrow
March 30, 1960

340
Bill Johnson with the Gene
Lowery Singers
Bobaloo
Bad Times Ahead
March 30, 1960

341
Sonny Wilson with the Gene
Lowery Singers
The Great Pretender
I'm Gonna Take a Walk
August 1, 1960

342
Bobbie Jean and the Ernie Barton
Orchestra
You Burned Bridges
Cheaters Never Win
July 7, 1960

343
Johnny Cash and the Tennessee Two
The Story of a Broken Heart
Down the Street to 301
July 14, 1960

344
Jerry Lee Lewis and His
Pumping Piano
John Henry
Hang Up My Rock and Roll Shoes
August 1, 1960

345
Tracy Pendarvis and the Swampers
Is It Me
South Bound Line
August 15, 1960

346
Bill Strength
Senorita
Guess I'd Better Go
September 12, 1960

347
Johnny Cash and the Tennessee Two
Mean Eyed Cat
Port of Lonely Hearts
October 1960

348
Lance Roberts with The Gene
Lowery Singers
The Good Guy Always Wins
The Time Is Right
October 1960

349
Tony Rossini with the Gene
Lowery Singers
I Gotta Know (Where I Stand)
Is It Too Late (to Say I'm Sorry)
November 14, 1960

350
The Rockin' Stockings
Yulesville U.S.A.
Rockin' Old Lang Syne
November 14, 1960
Note: Also issued as Sun 1960

351
Ira Jay II
You Don't Love Me
More Than Anything (in the World)
November 14, 1960

352
Jerry Lee Lewis with His
Pumping Piano
When I Get Paid
Love Made a Fool of Me
November 14, 1960

353
Roy Orbison
Sweet and Easy to Love
Devil Doll
November 25, 1960
Note: Reissue of Sun 265

354
Bobby Sheridan
Sad News
(with The Gene Lowery Singers)
Red Man
December 10, 1960

355
Johnny Cash and the Tennessee Two
Oh Lonesome Me
(with The Gene Lowery Singers)
Life Goes On
December 10, 1960

356
Jerry Lee Lewis and His
Pumping Piano
What'd I Say
Livin' Lovin' Wreck
February 27, 1961

357
Unissued

358
George Klein
U.T. Party Part I
U.T. Party Part II
March 10, 1961

359
Tracy Pendarvis
Belle of the Suwannee
Eternally
April 25, 1961

360
Wade Cagle and the Escorts
Groovy Train
Highland Rock
April 25, 1961

361
Anita Wood
I'll Wait Forever
I Can't Show How I Feel
June 25, 1961

362
Harold Dorman
I'll Stick By You
There They Go
May 21, 1961

363
Johnny Cash and the Tennessee Two
Sugartime
My Treasurer
May 21, 1961

364
Jerry Lee Lewis and His
Pumping Piano
Cold, Cold Heart
It Won't Happen with Me
May 26, 1961

365
Shirley Sisk
I Forgot to Remember to Forget
Other Side
August 1961

366
Tony Rossini
Well I Ask Ya
Darlena
August 1961

367
Jerry Lee Lewis and His
Pumping Piano
Save the Last Dance For Me
As Long As I Live
September 1, 1961

368
Don Hosea
Since I Met You
Uh Huh Unh
October 9, 1961

369
Bobby Wood
Everybody's Searching
Human Emotions
October 9, 1961
Note: Sun 369 probably unissued

370
Harold Dorman
Uncle Jonah's Place
Just One Step
November 7, 1961

371
Jerry Lee Lewis and His
Pumping Piano
Money
Bonnie B
November 21, 1961

372
Ray Smith
Travelin' Salesman
I Won't Miss You (Till You Go)
November 21, 1961

373
Rayburn Anthony
How Well I Know
Big Dream
January 19, 1962

374
Jerry Lee Lewis and His
Pumping Piano
I've Been Twistin'
Ramblin' Rose
January 19, 1962

375
Ray Smith
Candy Doll
Hey, Boss Man (Twist)
February 9, 1962

376
Johnny Cash and the Tennessee Two
Blue Train
Born to Lose
April 27, 1962

377
Harold Dorman
In the Beginning
Wait 'Til Saturday Night
April 4, 1962

378
Tony Rossini
(Meet Me) After School
Just Around the Corner
April 4, 1962

379
Jerry Lee Lewis
Sweet Little Sixteen
How's My Ex Treating You
July 7, 1962

380
Tony Rossini and the Chippers
You Make It Sound So Easy
New Girl in Town
July 10, 1962

381
The Four Upsetters
Crazy Arms
Midnight Soiree
November 5, 1962

382
Jerry Lee Lewis
Good Golly Miss Molly
I Can't Trust Me (in Your Arms Anymore)
November 5, 1962

383
Assigned to Johnny Cash but
not issued

384
Jerry Lee Lewis (with Linda Gail
Lewis)
Teenage Letter
Seasons of My Heart
April 1963

385
Linda Gail Lewis
Nothin' Shakin' (But the Leaves on the Trees)
Sittin' and Thinkin'
Note: Sun 365 unissued

386
The Four Upsetters
Surfin' Calliope
Wabash Cannonball
July 15, 1963

387
Tony Rossini
Nobody
Moved to Kansas City
July 15, 1963

388
The Teenangels
Ain't Gonna Let You (Break My Heart)
Tell Me My Love
Note: Only issued as promos

389
Billy Adams
Betty and Dupree
Got My Mojo Workin'
January 1, 1964

390
Bill Yates and His T-Birds
Don't Step on My Dog
Stop, Wait and Listen
May 1, 1964

Sun Records: The Singles (Continued)

391
Billy Adams with Jesse Carter
Trouble in Mind
Lookin' For Mary Ann
May 1, 1964

392
Johnny Cash & The Tennessee Three
Wide Open Road
Belshazah
May 1, 1964

393
Smokey Joe
Listen to Me Baby
The Signifying Monkey
May 1, 1964

394
Billy Adams
Reconsider Baby
Ruby Jane
September 1964

395
Randy and The Radiants
Peek-A-Boo
Mountain's High
January 1965

396
Jerry Lee Lewis
Carry Me Back to Old Virginia
I Know What It Means
March 15, 1965

397
Gorgeous Bill
Carleen
Too Late to Right My Wrong
March 15, 1965

398
Randy and the Radiants
My Way of Thinking
Truth From My Eyes
November 25, 1965

399
Bill Yates
Big Big World
I Dropped My M & M's
February 1, 1966

400
The Jesters
My Babe
Cadillac Man
February 1, 1966

401
Billy Adams
Open the Door Richard
Rock Me Baby
February 1, 1966

402
Dane Stinit
Don't Knock What You Don't
Understand
Always On the Go
May 1966

403
David Houston
Sherry's Lips
Miss Brown
October 10, 1966
Reissue of Phillips International 3583

404
The Climates
No You for Me
Breaking Up Again
February 1967

405
Dane Stinit
Sweet Country Girl
That Muddy Ole River (Near
Memphis, Tennessee)
February 1967

406
Brother James Anderson
I'm Gonna Move in the Room
with the Lord
I'm Tired, My Soul Needs Resting
February 1967
Issued as "Gospel Series"

407
Load of Mischief
Back in My Arms Again
I'm a Lover
January 1968

Sun Records: The EPs
EPA series

101
Johnny Cash

102
Johnny Cash

103
Johnny Cash
Note: 101-103 advertised as available in
October 1957 but most likely not issued.

104
Jerry Lee Lewis
(Tentative compilation)

105
Jerry Lee Lewis
(Tentative compilation)

106
Jerry Lee Lewis
(Tentative compilation)
Note: 104-106 not issued.

107
Jerry Lee Lewis
The Great Ball of Fire

108
Jerry Lee Lewis
Jerry Lee Lewis
June 1958

109
Jerry Lee Lewis
Jerry Lee Lewis
June 1958

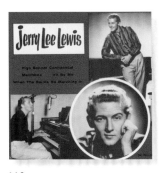

110
Jerry Lee Lewis
Jerry Lee Lewis
June 1958

111
Johnny Cash
Sings Hank Williams
June 1958

112
Johnny Cash
Johnny Cash

113
Johnny Cash
I Walk the Line

114
Johnny Cash
His Top Hits

115
Carl Perkins
Blue Suede Shoes

116
Johnny Cash
Home of the Blues

117
Johnny Cash
So Doggone Lonesome
April 1960

Sun Records; The LPs

The LP/SLP Series

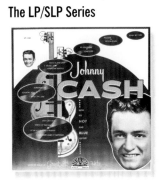

1220
Johnny Cash
With His Hot and Blue Guitar!
November 1957

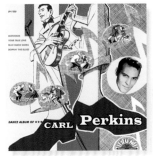

1225
Carl Perkins
Dance Album of…
1958
Note: Reissued in 1960 with different jacket as "*Teen Beat*"

1230
Jerry Lee Lewis
Jerry Lee Lewis
June 1958

1235
Johnny Cash
Sings the Songs That Made Him Famous
November 1958

1240
Johnny Cash
Greatest!
October 1959

THE COMPLETE SUN DISCOGRAPHY
(Continued)

Sun Records: The LPs (Continued)

1245
Johnny Cash
Sings Hand Williams and Other Favorite Tunes
July 1960

1250
Various Artists
Million Sellers
1961
Note: Reissued with different jacket as *Sun's Gold Hits, Volume 1.*

1255
Johnny Cash
Now Here's Johnny Cash
October 1961

1260
Roy Orbison
At the Rock House
1961

1265
Jerry Lee Lewis
Jerry Lee's Greatest!
1961

1270
Johnny Cash
All Aboard the Blue Train
November 1962

1275
Johnny Cash
Original Sun Sound of Johnny Cash
November 1964

The Flip Label:
The Singles

501
Carl Perkins
Movie Magg
Turn Around
February 1955

502
Bill Taylor—Clyde Leoppard's Snearly Ranch Boys
Lonely Sweetheart
Bill Taylor and Smokey Jo—Clyde Leoppard's Snearly Ranch Boys
Split Personality
February 1955

503
Charlie Feathers
I've Been Deceived
Peepin' Eyes
March 1955

504
The Miller Sisters
Someday You Will Pay
You Didn't Think I Would
April 1955

Note: Flip 503 and 504 were reissued as Sun 503 and 504, after legal action from the Flip label in Los Angeles. Sun 227, 228, 231, and 237 were also issued with the same catalogue numbers on Flip Records.

Phillips International:
The Singles

3516
Buddy Blake
You Passed Me By
Please Convince Me
September 1957

3517
Hayden Thompson
Love My Baby
One Broken Heart
September 1957

3518
Barbara Pittman
Two Young Fools In Love
I'm Getting Better All the Time
September 1957

3519
Bill Justis and His Orchestra
Raunchy
Midnight Man
September 1957

3520
Johnny Carroll
That's the Way I Love
I'll Wait
September 1957

3521
Cliff Thomas
Treat Me Right
I'm On the Way Home
January 1958

3522
Bill Justis and His Orchestra
College Man
The Stranger (Vocal by The Spinners)
February 1958

3523
Wayne Powers
My Love Song
Point of View
March 1958

3524
Bill Pinky and the Turks
After the Hop
Sally's Got a Sister
March 1958

3525
Bill Justis and His Orchestra
Wild Rice
Scroungie
March 1958

3526
Carl McVoy
You Are My Sunshine
Tootsie
May 1958

3527
Barbara Pittman with the
Bill Justis Orchestra
Cold, Cold Heart
Everlasting Love
June 1958

3528
Ernie Barton
Stairway of Love
Raining the Blues
June 1958

3529
Bill Justis and His Orchestra
Cattywampus
Summer Holiday
June 1958

3530
Lee Mitchell
The Frog
A Little Bird Told Me
September 1958

3531
Cliff Thomas, Ed, and Barbara
Sorry I Lied
Leave It to Me
September 1958

3532
Charlie Rich
Whirlwind
Philadelphia Baby
October 1958

3533
Mickey Milan with the Bill
Justis Orchestra
*Somehow Without You (with the
Montclairs)*
The Picture (with Chorus)
September 1958

3534
Ken Cook
Crazy Baby
I Was a Fool
October 1958

3535
Bill Justis and His Orchestra
Bop Train
String of Pearls—Cha Hot Cha
October 1958

3536
The Clement Travelers
The Minstrel Show
Three Little Guitars
February 1959

3537
Jimmy Demopoulos
Hopeless Love
If I Had My Baby
February 1959

3538
Cliff Thomas, Ed, and Barbara
I'm the Only One
Tidewind
March 1959

3539
Carl Mann
Mona Lisa
Foolish One
March 1959

3540
Edwin Howard
Forty-'Leven Times
More Pretty Girls Than One
April 1959

3541
Ernie Barton
Open the Door Richard
Shut Your Mouth
1959

3542
Charlie Rich
Rebound
Big Man
June 1959

3543
Bobbie and the Boys
To Tell the Truth
Silly Blues
June 1959

3544
Bill Justis and His Orchestra
Flea Circus
Cloud Nine
July 1959

3545
Brad Suggs
706 Union
Low Outside
September 1959

3546
Carl Mann
Rockin' Love
Pretend
September 1959

3547
Memphis Bells
The Midnight Whistle
Snow Job
October 1959

3548
Mack Self
Mad at You
Willie Brown
October 1959

3549
Brad Suggs and the Orchestra
and Chorus
I Walk the Line
Ooh-Wee
October 1959

3550
Carl Mann
Some Enchanted Evening
I Can't Forget
January 1960

THE COMPLETE SUN DISCOGRAPHY
(Continued)

3551
Sonny Burgess
Sadie's Back in Town
Kiss Goodnight
January 1960

3552
Charlie Rich with the Gene Lowery
Chorus
Lonely Weekends
Everything I Do Is Wrong
January 1960

3553
Barbara Pittman with The Gene
Lowery Singers
The Eleventh Commandment
Handsome Man
April 1960

3554
Brad Suggs with the Gene Lowery
Chorus
Cloudy
Partly Cloudy
April 1960

3555
Carl Mann with the Gene Lowery
Chorus
South of the Border
I'm Comin' Home
May 1960

3556
Don Hinton with the Gene Lowery
Chorus
Jo Ann
Honey Bee
May 1960

3557
Jeb Stewart with the Gene
Lowery Singers
Sunny Side of the Street
Take a Chance
June 1960

3558
Eddie Bush with The Gene
Lowery Singers
Baby I Don't Care
Vanished
June 1960

3559
The Hawk
In the Mood
I Get the Blues When it Rains
August 1960

3560
Charlie Rich with the Gene
Lowery Singers
School Days
Gonna Be Waiting
May 1960

3561
Danny Stewart
Somewhere Along the Line
I'll Change My Ways
August 1960

3562
Charlie Rich
On My Knees
Stay
September 7, 1960

3563
Brad Suggs
My Gypsy
Sam's Tune
October 13, 1960

3564
Carl Mann
Wayward Wind
Born to Be Bad
March 11, 1961

3565
Jimmy Louis
Your Fool
Gone and Left Me Blues
November 11, 1961

3566
Charlie Rich
Who Will the Next Fool Be
Caught in the Middle
February 24, 1961

3567
Jeb Stuart
Dream
Come Down with the Blues
April 28, 1961

3568
Nelson Ray
You're Everything
You've Come Home
April 28, 1961

3569
Carl Mann
If I Could Change You
I Ain't Got No Home
July 1961

3570
Jean Dee
My Greatest Hurt
Nothing Down (99 Years to Pay)
July 1961

3571
Brad Suggs—Orchestra and Chorus
Elephant Walk
Catching Up
November 1961

3572
Charlie Rich
Just a Little Bit Sweet
It's Too Late
September 1961

3573
Mikki Wilcox
I Know What It Means
Willing and Waiting
September 1961

3574
Freddie North
Don't Make Me Cry
Sometime She'll Come Along
October 1961

3575
Jeb Stuart
I Betcha Gonna Like It
Little Miss Love
February 1962

3576
Charlie Rich
Easy Money
Midnight Blues
April 1962

3577
Thomas Wayne
I've Got It Made
The Quiet Look
April 1962

3578
Frank Frost and the Night Hawks
Crawlback
Jelly Roll King
June 1962

3579
Carl Mann
When I Grow Too Old to Dream
Mountain Dew
June 1962

3580
Jeb Stuart and The Chippers
I Ain't Never
In Love Again
June 1962

3581
David Wilkins
Thanks a Lot
There's Something About You
June 1962

3582
Charlie Rich
Sittin' and Thinkin'
Finally Found Out
October 1962

3583
David Houston
Sherry's Lips
Miss Brown
1963

3584
Charlie Rich
There's Another Place I Can't Go
I Need Your Love
1963

3585
Jeanne Newman
The Boy I Met Today
Thanks a Lot
1963

3586
The Quintones
Times Sho' Gettin' Ruff
Softie
1963

Phillips International:
The LPs
PILP or PLP Series

1950
Bill Justis and His Orchestra
Cloud Nine (Far Out Tunes by Bill Justis and His Orchestra)
August 1960

1955
Graham Forbes and the Trio
The Martini Set
August 1960

1960
Carl Mann
Like, Mann
August 1960

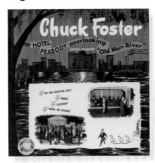

1965
Chuck Foster
*Hotel Peabody Overlooking
Old Man River*
August 1960

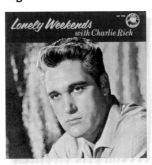

1970
Charlie Rich
Lonely Weekends with Charlie Rich
August 1960

1975
Frank Frost with the Night Hawks
Hey Boss Man!
1962

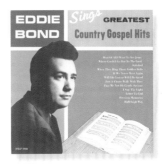

1980
Eddie Bond
Sings Greatest Country Gospel Hits
1962

1985
Frank Ballard with Phillip
Reynold's Band
Rhythm Blues Party
1962

ACKNOWLEDGMENTS

Primary Wave

Thanks to: Larry Mestel, Ramon Villa, Bill Cisneros, Dominic Pandiscia, Robert Dippold, Donna Grecco, Adam Lowenberg, Justin Shukat, Marty Silverstone, Jeff Straughn, Sam Sklover, Catie Monck, Sean Lewis, Natalia Nastaskin, Amy Ortner, Sam Rhulen, Jane Reisman, and all at Primary Wave Music; Jerry Lee Lewis, Peter Guralnick, Colin Escott, John Singleton, Chase Gregory, Adrienne Kelley, Laura Pochodylo, Tracey Green, and the entire Sun Records team; Paul Sizelove, Meghann Wright, Emmie Chambers, Melissa Chambers, Melissa Miller, Matthew Beckett and all at Sun Label Group; Michelle Jubelirer, Jacqueline Saturn, Matt Sawn and all at Virgin Label Services/UMG; Norman Perry, Rick Smith, Reney Palome, Ellen Pugliese and all at Perryscope Productions; Dawn Kamerling and all at The Press House; Josh Matas, Jerry Phillips, Chris Isaak, and Sheryl Louis; the Sun Diner team; Matt Abruzzo, German Roman, and all at Authentic Brands Group; Roger Shaw, Raoul Goff, Karyn Gerhard, James Faccinto and all at Weldon Owen and Weldon Owen/Insight Editions; Paul and Cynthia Rogers, David Spero, Jonas Herbsman, Kelly Pribble, and the Iron Mountain team.

Colin Escott

Sam Phillips quotations and background from interviews by Martin Hawkins; Hank Davis and Colin Escott; Elizabeth Deane (WGBH, funded by the Grammy Foundation (R)); Elizabeth Kaye (*Rolling Stone*, February 13, 1986); Barbara Schultz (*Mix* magazine, October 1, 2000); Robert Palmer (Memphis magazine, December 1978). And of course, Peter Guralnick's definitive biography, *Sam Phillips—The Man Who Invented Rock 'n' Roll* (Little, Brown/Back Bay, 2015).

Weldon Owen

Deepest thanks and gratitude go to: Dominic Pandiscia, Robert Dippold, and everyone at Primary Wave for making this possible; Jerry Lee Lewis for his thoughtful Foreword; all of the collectors and archivists who generously contributed their amazing images to the book, including Jerry Phillips and Jim Jaworowicz at the Phillips Collection, Donna Grecco for Primary Wave, John Boija, Bill Greensmith, Dave Booth, Sylvia Pitcher, Matt Abruzzo at Authentic Brands Group, Greg Johnson at Ole Miss, and Rachel Morris at MTSU; our designer Roger Gorman, copyeditor Bob Cooper, proofreader Jessica Easto, and indexer Kevin O'Connor; and finally, to our authors, Peter Guralnick and Colin Escott, whose knowledge, extraordinary talent, and unending willingness to go over and above have made this book a true treasure.

Scan and listen to the essential Sun Records Playlist

PHOTO CREDITS

The publisher wishes to thank the following for the generous use of their images in this book.

All paper record labels that appear in this book (with the exception of p.103) are from the collection of John Boija.

(Key: R=right; L=left; M=middle; T=top; B=bottom, I=inset; Col=column)
The John Boija Collection: 14, 15, 17, 18, 19, 39, 57, 61, 63, 64, 69, 71, 72, 75, 77, 78, 81, 83, 84, 89, 91, 92T, 95, 96, 98, 100, 104T, 106, 109, 111, 112all, 115, 117, 118, 121T, 125, 126T, 129, 131, 132, 135, 136T, 138, 141, 142all, 145, 147T, 148, 150T, 153, 155T, 156, 159T, 161all, 164, 167, 169T, 170, 172T, 175T, 177, 178, 179I, 181, 183T, 184, 185I, 186T, 189, 190, 192, 195 ,196, 198, 199, 201, 202, 205, 224, 237, 238, 242all, 243Col1all, 243Col2all, 243Col3M, 243Col3T, 244Col1B, 247Col2B, 247Col4all; Billy Emerson/and more bears: 94; Colin Escott: 4, 5, 10, 12, 14, 17, 20, 24, 30, 31, 32, 33, 37,42B, 42T, 44-5, 46, 47, 49, 50-1, 54-55, 58, 59, 60, 68, 70, 74, 76, 82-3, 88, 90, 92B, 94, 99, 101, 104B, 107, 107I, 110, 116, 119, 121B, 128, 130, 133I, 134, 136B, 137, 139, 140, 144, 147B, 149, 149I, 157,159B, 165, 168, 173, 182, 183B, 185, 188, 191, 194, 200, 203, 204; The Colin Escott Collection, Center for Popular Music, Middle Tennessee State University: 113; The Sheldon Harris Collection, University of Mississippi Libraries: 65; Bill Greensmith: 52-3; Bill Greensmith, Blues Unlimited: 127; Phillips Archive: 4, 7, 11, 13T, 13B, 16, 21, 23, 28, 29, 34-5, 40-1, 48, 154, 187, 197, 230, 150B, 155B, 175B, 188I, 232-3; Elvis Presley Entertainment: 8-9, 66-7, 114, 120, 124, 133, Photofest: 43R; Sylvia Pitcher Photo Library: 73; The Doug Seroff African American Gospel Quartet Collection, Center for Popular Music, Middle Tennessee State University: 102; Showtime: 2-3, 4, 6, 22, 26, 27, 36, 56, 56I, 85, 86-7, 93, 108, 122-3, 146, 151, 152, 162-3, 171, 174, 176, 179, 180, 180I, 193, 206-7; Courtesy of Sun Label Group, LLC: 39, 43L, 44, 80, 158, 160, 166, 169B, 173I, 208-9, 210, 211, 212-13, 214-15, 216, 217, 218all, 219, 220, 221all, 222all, 223all, 225all, 226all, 227, 228, 243Col3B, 243Col 4all, 244Col1M, 244Col 1T, 244Col2all, 247Col2T, 247Col3all; © Dr. Ernest C. Withers, Sr. courtesy of the WITHERS FAMILY TRUST: 62, 79, 143.

All best efforts have been made to identify and secure permissions for images.

Lyric Credits

"Boogie Disease," "Seems Like a Million Years," and "Time Has Made a Change," lyrics are reprinted with permission from Hi-Lo Music.

INDEX

INDEX

INDEX

weldon**owen**

an imprint of Insight Editions
P.O. Box 3088
San Rafael, CA 94912
www.weldonowen.com

CEO Raoul Goff
VP Publisher Roger Shaw
Editorial Director Katie Killebrew
Senior Editor Karyn Gerhard
VP Creative Chrissy Kwasnik
Art Director Allister Fein
VP Manufacturing Alix Nicholaeff
Production Manager Joshua Smith
Sr Production Manager, Subsidiary Rights Lina s Palma-Temena

Design by Roger Gorman, Reiner Design Consultants, Inc

ISBN: 978-1-68188-896-5

Manufactured in China by Insight Editions
10 9 8 7 6 5 4 3 2 1

Insight Editions, in association with Roots of Peace, will plant two trees for each tree used in the manufacturing
of this book. Roots of Peace is an internationally renowned humanitarian organization dedicated to eradicating
land mines worldwide and converting war-torn lands into productive farms and wildlife habitats. Roots of Peace
will plant two million fruit and nut trees in Afghanistan and provide farmers there with the skills and support
necessary for sustainable land use.